Through the Fog

Navigating life's challenges
while raising kids with hearing loss

Valli Gideons

Copyright © 2022 Valli Gideons

All rights reserved. No part of this book may be reproduced or used in any manner without written permission of the copyright owner except for the use of quotations in a book review.
For more information, email the author at gideonsbook@gmail.com
FIRST EDITION
ISBN: 9798485694470

www.mybattlecall.com

My Why

For Battle & Harper,

Being your mother has been
the greatest honor of my life.

For anyone who is working through grief,
in need of life-saving grace,
looking for a sliver of hope,

Even from the trenches, never stop believing.

~ Valli Gideons ~

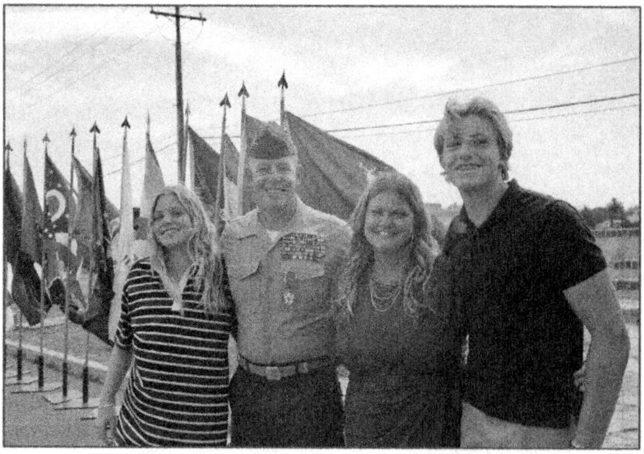

Contents

	Introduction	*vii*
1	Introducing Bob	1
2	Big Dreams	7
3	The Fog	13
4	Words I Hated	23
5	The Dreaded Whistle	29
6	Grace	35
7	The Gift	39
8	Eye Rolls	43
9	The Bean	53
10	Rainbow Connection	59
11	Lost at Sea	65
12	Magic Moments	71

13	Cancer: A Good One	75
14	Those Damn Boots	81
15	Hard Things	89
16	I am Here	103
17	In the Trenches	113
18	Maker of the Home	119
19	Rituals	123
20	No Place Like Home	129
21	Horseshoes	135
22	To My Child's New IEP Team	141
23	Dear Insurance Company	145
24	Standing Ovation	151
25	My Battle Call	155

26	To My Daughter	163
27	About Teens	169
28	The Mustache	175
29	Perspective	179
30	New Season	183
31	Things I Learned Being a Military Bride	187
32	Dear Me	191
	Glossary of Terms	*199*
	Bonus Section	*205*

"This book weaves together beautifully the significant hardships of raising two children with hearing loss with pieces about things like marriage and work and friendships, and in doing so it reminds the reader how we are ALL the sum of our parts and not just our struggles.

Valli meets us where we are—which so often is knee deep in the struggle—but then also reminds us of ALL of the other pieces of who we are and what our life is, because the struggle is not who we are. The life is, all of it. And this book reflects a life, not just a series of struggles. It reads like a path forward."

—Liz Petrone, Author of *The Price of Admission*

Introduction

Before Google, before Facebook, way, way back when AOL pretty much owned email exclusively, two blondes walked into a journalism classroom. One was from the beachy East Coast, one was from the beachy West Coast, and they joked about being "The 'V' Girls" because of the initials of their first names.

That's it, friends.

The punchline, if you were looking for one, is how time flies and paths weave their way back over themselves and bring us to what you're holding in your hands.

Valli and I both fled the English department in college and found ourselves in the presence of a guy you'll hear about in the upcoming pages, Dr. R, with his beloved green pen, and here I am, all these years later, blessed and humbled to write a few words about the lovely, awesome essays you're about to read.

While I stayed planted in the Mid-Atlantic as a long-time Navy spouse and became a journalist, Valli, a Marine Corps newlywed, uprooted as she would do many more times to come, and started writing about her adventures as the Internet blossomed, then exploded, and opened up so many different platforms for her to reach people.

First through email, then on Facebook, Valli and I touched base as much as we could as our lives changed, diverged, and came back together when she put out tentative feelers about starting a blog when her son was diagnosed with hearing loss. We both loved the idea of her calling it, *My Battle Call*.

First posts were about those difficult early years—the typical new mom challenges amplified by the needs of her newly-diagnosed newborn, the deployments of her husband, and the distance from friends and family.

Like some of those early pieces, these essays demonstrate Valli's indefatigable grit, necessary for any military bride, but also how it grew, how she became a staunch advocate for accessibility, and a firm believer in—and an ample giver of her trademark—grace—while she connected with others in the Deaf/Hard of Hearing communities and built a solid, widespread network that came to include other popular mom-bloggers who have become close friends and allies.

From a distance, I shared the journey you're about to read of the obstacles Valli met and overcame—cancer; a second child born with hearing loss; deployment "single" parenthood; and move after move across the country.

These pages contain the good times and bad, relayed with Valli's characteristic humor and adherence to delivering truth without the sugarcoating, but with the awareness that our strongest assets—integrity, self-awareness, and above everything else, love—can bring us to a place of acceptance and peace, even when it might hurt a little to get there, and recognizing the safest places to land can be in the arms and homes of friends and chosen family, when we may have lost loved ones along the way.

As her children have entered their teen years and new challenges await (and as any parent of teenagers knows, many have already arrived), Valli's attention to advocacy is what directed her to share her story with a larger audience, prompted by learning after a speaking engagement that professionals in the medical community were shocked by some of the things she shared that happened when her children were first diagnosed. These professionals, she told me, didn't want to make the same insensitive mistakes.

No spoilers, but ahead are tips and tricks and things Valli wished she had known, gentle guidance, hard-earned wisdom, laughter, and some beautiful reflections that might be a bit bittersweet.

Whether you've been there for a while or are new to the hearing loss community, Valli's words will resonate.

I was honored to help with Valli's first book project with her daughter, Harper, in *Now Hear This: Harper Soars with her Magic Ears*. I'm equally honored and thrilled to contribute my efforts to this one.

It's been a long time since we roller-bladed down the boardwalk, appeared on local news together, walked out exhausted from a mind-bending movie or two, and sat together gleaning writerly wisdom from our cherished Dr. R. (And I'm so grateful that English 111 turned out not to be our thing!) We gained a lot from those classes, but the best was this friendship.

My admiration, respect, and love for this woman has only grown over the distance and the years, and I guarantee you'll find the same reasons in these pages to understand why I'm not the only one who feels that way when encountering this remarkable human.

Veni Fields, January 2022

1

Introducing Bob

When I was in second grade, I wrote a short story about a walking, talking sponge named Bob. My teacher, Mrs. Shem, had red hair and smelled like lavender. She told me my story was a masterpiece. Her encouragement and belief in my words gave me the fuel to keep writing.

I am not sure how the now infamous cartoon ever came to fruition, but I do know I never received a dime. Nonetheless, I continued to have a deep love for writing throughout my teen years. Insatiably, I scribbled in journals; years later I transitioned to writing on a word processor with no spell-check or cut-and-paste features. I was compelled to tell stories.

Next. I entered a liberal arts university and my freshman year I got a "C" in English literature.

I nearly drowned from all the red ink spread across the pages on the first paper I wrote.

My professor, a transplant from New York full of sophistication, wore expensive shoes and made me feel small. She found a hundred different ways to criticize my "journalistic" style. It was excruciating. She loved the romantic classics. I preferred the likes of Capote and Ross.

I put my creative pen away.

Only, luck would have it when I stumbled upon a class called 101 Journalism and registered for it, mostly because I needed the credit and the time of day fit my schedule.

It was in *that* class I would meet a male version of Mrs. Shem.

Dr. R read my words with enthusiasm, used

green ink, and insisted I do this writing thing because in his words, I had *"the right stuff."*

He wore wrinkled ties, his bifocals hung off his nose crookedly, and his hair was always slightly disheveled. He wrote a column in the city newspaper, was unassuming and humble, and had an office with bookcases overflowing from floor to ceiling. He suggested I give writing for the school newspaper a try.

I must have had half a dozen or more classes with him during my time in college. And even though Dr. R always used a lot of green ink, he also used words like *"YES!"* and *"Spectacular choice."*

Sprinkled in his edits were corrections and suggestions, but he always led with a positive comment.

A real teacher and mentor, he invested in young writers. Those of us who were lucky enough to find ourselves on his roster were part of a *Dead Poet's Society* of sorts.

To this day, I think about him when I make specific stylistic choices. I can still hear him encouraging me to use my own voice, tell my story, take chances and risks.

I went on to earn my own byline, working for a magazine after graduation, eventually getting a weekly column of my own. Then, life changed. I put the chapter of "professional writer" on hold.

✴

Fast forward: years later I was on a girls' weekend with my lifelong besties from elementary school, Nancy and Belinda. By now the three of us were married and had kids, but we managed to escape for an annual trip together. While lying poolside at a swanky resort, we chatted about dreams and goals, old times and the daily grind. They asked me why I didn't write anymore. I really didn't know. I guess in the trenches of motherhood, I didn't think I had any new stories to tell. My friends made a case for why they thought I was wrong.

Once I returned home from the getaway, the conversation that took place on those chaise lounges kept marinating. I began the steps to launch my blog, *My Battle Call.*

Perhaps I *did* have more stories to tell. Nancy and Belinda's belief in me gave me the courage to pick my pen back up and start using my own voice again.

Years later, I feel like that second-grade girl who wrote stories with unabashed freedom and joy. It is such an honor to share words some find encouraging while also providing a sliver of hope. Instead of ever receiving credit for the cartoon about that sponge, I went on to write a children's book with my daughter about her hearing loss. Isn't life funny that way?

It's exactly the way it was meant to be. And somehow all those years of scribbling led me to this place. I didn't know it way back then, but perhaps I'd been writing this next chapter since my days in that first journalism class. Maybe Dr. R was right, there really is a new story to tell if you are willing to take risks and use your own voice.

All these years later, I am hitting publish *again* while patiently waiting for an update about my royalties on that dang sponge.

2

Big Dreams

We started dating and 5 months later my dad died. My then-boyfriend, Chris, showed up to Dad's funeral in full military dress blues. I knew then he was a keeper.

A month later Chris deployed to Somalia. There were no cell phones, no emails, no FaceTimes. We wrote love letters, which would often take months to arrive.

On the rare occasion I would be home to catch

a call when he randomly found a pay phone, we'd be lucky to have 5 minutes to talk before it was the next guy's turn in line to phone home.

Nothing was more heartbreaking than returning home to a missed call on my answering machine; I played those messages over and over again.

We would marry in our favorite beach town a little more than three years after meeting in the one of the cheesiest San Diego bars with my childhood friend, Nancy, still by my side.

We moved across the country two days after we returned from our honeymoon. Our car was filled with everything we owned, and our hearts were full of big dreams.

✷

When we were finally fortunate enough to have our first child, after experiencing a devastating miscarriage, we found out two weeks after our son was delivered that he was born with severe hearing loss. Twenty-two months later, our daughter would also be born with the same.

Ten deployments, ten moves, and two kids later, we returned to our cherished beach town. Chris recently retired from military service here, surrounded by many of the people who joined us on our wedding day and many of whom we've served with around the globe.

Talk about full circle moments.

✷

Those big dreams? We met with a military financial counselor when we were snot-nosed kids, just newly engaged. He told us to imagine ourselves when we were "old, like forty."

Where did we want to be?

Right here: so many of those big dreams coming true, dropping anchor in our favorite beach town, toes in the sand, ocean breezes across our faces. We had no idea *hearing loss* would be part of our parenting journey. Being faced with having a child with any kind of disability can be the death of a marriage. Each person experiences the diagnosis differently and processes the grief, anger, denial, and acceptance at varying paces. You can become a stronger team; or sadly, the gravity of it all can tear you apart. We almost lost our bearings, buried under the weight of it.

Luckily we found our way into a couple's therapy room. The therapist had us do a simple yet profound exercise. Our task was to make a list of things we loved about each other and then bring it to the following session. Having procrastinated, an hour before our follow-up session, my heart began to pour out love language onto a page. Once I started, I couldn't stop.

It wasn't the big things that resonated. Instead, it was the nuances, tidbits in a mental walk down memory lane, and all his beloved other idiosyncrasies I loved and had stopped noticing. I still have that list tucked safely inside an old journal. I take it out and read it from time to time; that scrap of paper was a relationship-saver of sorts and one of my most treasured possessions. What resonated the most for both of us were the little things.

It was evident as I read my list to him, tears streaming down my cheeks, that he heard me. His face softened in a way that had become the exception rather than the norm.

Then he shared his list with me. Be still, my heart. The abundant amount of thoughtfulness in the details woke me up. In his list were nuances only someone with whom you share a history, a deep friendship, and a deep love, would understand. It was one of the many times I realized ours was a relationship worthy of a rescue strategy.

✳

This has not been an easy life. We haven't had total bliss. But here's the thing: I don't think that's the way of it. Marriage and building a family together is hard work, which is what makes the *sticking* part that much sweeter.

We have built a solid life together; All these years later, we are still riding.

Still chasing big dreams.

3

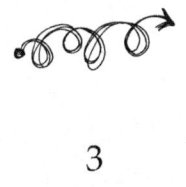

The Fog

When the stick turned blue on the drug store pregnancy test, we were elated. We had waited several years to begin our family, and we were so ready for this next season in our lives to begin. My mother-in-law took me shopping for maternity clothes at the posh maternity store, A Pea in the Pod, when I was only four weeks along—even though I wasn't showing at all.

Our baby was going to be her first grandchild.

I couldn't wait to grow into those clothes.

In the evenings, we sometimes lay in bed with a speaker placed on my belly, playing classical music by Mozart or Chopin because we had read it was good for the baby's brain.

We thought about possible names, imagining what color hair and eyes our baby would have, and we started buying onesies.

*

At twelve weeks, we went in for a routine ultrasound. It was then we learned the unimaginable. As the cold wand moved back and forth across my tummy, there was no heartbeat detected.

A surge of grief washed over me like nothing I had ever experienced.

We had been warned not to share with everyone that we were expecting until we were "in the clear," but we were unable to silence our excitement. And we had never imagined this.

My doctor and I discussed my options.

The next morning my husband took me to

check into the hospital for the procedure. My mom jumped on a plane from the West Coast, rushing to be with us for what would be a painful aftermath. Because in a time like *this,* all I knew for sure is that I wanted my mom by my side.

There were no meal trains or local prayer circles because we had recently been stationed hundreds of miles from the nearest military base, and we hadn't yet had the opportunity to make any friends at this new remote duty station.

My doctor showed me a tremendous amount of compassion and grace. She knew it was one of my worst days even though she'd probably walked others through this so many times. It was an excruciatingly gut-wrenching experience, from start to finish.

Even now, over a decade and half later, I am thankful I had the support from my doctor and my mom.

Nonetheless, it was difficult. It still is.

So when months later, the next pregnancy stick turned blue—we were cautiously optimistic. We took three tests to be sure.

✶

He was named before he even entered the world. It "only" took my husband seven months to convince me that naming our baby boy "Battle" would be a good idea.

"Just think about it," Chris would say. *"Imagine, the announcer over the loudspeaker saying, 'Battle on the tackle.' The crowd would go wild."* He believed it might set the boy up for greatness.

I was eventually convinced that giving our child a name he would have to live up to might be a good idea. Kind of like the message in the Johnny Cash song "A Boy Named Sue." Names sometimes have a way of telling a story about a person or giving them something to live up to.

As my belly bump continued to grow, I began to experience the ubiquitous expectant-mother questions from strangers:

"Are you having a boy or a girl?"

"Do you have a name?"

"It's a boy," I would share. When I told them the name we were considering, inevitably their eyes would widen, looking perplexed. Next:

"What?"

"B-A-T-T-L-E" I would spell out. *"It is like rattle but with a B."*

As I had suspected during my initial hesitancy, people looked at me in disbelief, awkwardly shifting the conversation to things like car seats and breast milk or formula. My baby was still in the womb, and I was already feeling judged by others.

I quickly began to second-guess being talked into *this* name.

But the full-court press by my persistent husband continued. He knew deep down this name was it.

I have no idea why, but the name began to grow on me. Eventually, the hand-painted wood letters went up on the nursery walls. It was official. Our baby boy was well on his way. The writing was on the wall.

A few short weeks later, the tale to end all tales happened:

"Do you have a name?" a woman at the grocery store asked.

"Yes, it is Battle," I replied without hesitation.

"*It's a family name,*" I added.

The woman's ears perked up, leaning in as if to hear more.

"*He's actually named after my husband's Great Uncle Battle, who fought in the Civil War.*"

It was amazing. Just like that—my far-fetched story was received with immediate acceptance.

✵

Our due date finally arrived.

After fourteen hours of labor, our baby entered the world full of gusto. Then, still in a postpartum haze, we found out he had failed the routine infant hearing screening.

At the time, our baby failing something that was *routine* seemed like the least of our worries. This little person was coming home with us. Overnight, we became parents.

The hospital staff told us: It was probably *just fluid in the ear canal*…anyway.

We left the hospital with an appointment scheduled for the more extensive test, an Auditory Brain Response (ABR).

In the meantime, we took our son home and attempted to care for our new pint-sized roommate. Feed. Change. Soothe. Repeat. Nipple creams, diaper creams, so many things. After two weeks of sleepless nights, the day arrived for the follow-up test. We assumed we would leave the hospital that day with "all clear" results.

The audiologist informed us that our baby must hold perfectly still for at least an hour to get accurate readings. Simply nurse this crying, pooping machine to sleep, easy-peasy.

Sweat beads ran down my back while I tried to perform this task, stuck to the giant leather recliner designated for the parents of infants. Those in this department had seen this done many times. For us, it was like entering a foreign country, unable to speak the language.

My new mommy arms throbbed and started to go numb, as my baby was finally settled and falling asleep.

Oh, perfect: I had to pee. But there was *no way* I was going to move.

Sensors were placed on his tiny, scrunched-up

forehead. I studied his baby acne and perfect heart-shaped lips, while also struggling to keep the miniature earbuds and wires—leading to who knows where—inserted into his squishy little ears.

Our bodies were mushed. I was drenched. *"Please don't wake up,"* I prayed.

The audiologist took her place behind the glass. Frozen. We waited.

✷

Then: The Room. The cold, little space no parent wants an invitation to enter.

Dr. Lab Coat entered.

"Your son failed."

What?

Dr. Lab Coat said our baby's hearing loss was severe-to-profound, he would get hearing aids, may be a candidate for a cochlear implant, and probably go to mainstream high school.

Wait...

What? High School? Profound? A candidate for...

What?

Next thing we knew, follow-ups were scheduled with Ear, Nose, and Throat doctors (ENTs), audiologists, geneticists, and intervention specialists. It was all too much.

We bundled our baby up and headed out to battle Cleveland's lake-effect snow.

We wandered.

Where was that stupid car?

We searched the maze of a city-sized parking garage at this city-sized hospital.

When we had arrived hours earlier that day, we had no idea. We never imagined the outcome of the test would be *this*.

Our precious infant was clipped back in his car seat behind us. Then we just sat staring straight ahead.

There were no words.

We wept.

In that single moment, in that single morning, our journey of navigating through the fog began.

4

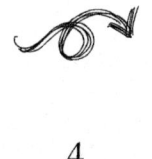

Words I Hated

When we returned home with our baby after receiving this unexpected diagnosis, everything we imagined changed. We went from *just* trying to figure out how to be new parents to worrying about becoming "experts" in something we knew nothing about. My baby was the first deaf person I had ever met.

While most of the people around us meant well, they often didn't know what to say or how to help.

"He will be fine," they said over and over again.

When our baby was initially diagnosed with hearing loss, I did not want to hear the word *fine*. Because, here's the thing: in those early days—it was not fine. None of it.

I was scared.

I was sad.

I was overwhelmed.

I was in shock.

I was worried.

I was grieving.

The word *fine* felt minimizing.

Being told it would be fine felt like being told to just "suck it up!" Deep down, I am sure I believed my son *would* be fine. But there would be so many steps we had to take to get there.

What I longed for was validation and acknowledgment of the gravity of what this meant. I wanted to be understood. I wanted my feelings to be affirmed. I didn't want or need to hear he would be fine.

In the beginning, I didn't want to be told in a

single breath that he would get hearing aids, possibly be a candidate for a cochlear implant, and probably go to mainstream high school.

Those statements made me feel ashamed to be experiencing grief. It made me feel embarrassed for feeling sad, like I should just buck up.

In those early stages, what I needed was empathy and compassion. I needed time to digest it all. I needed to move through the grieving process so I could come to a place of acceptance.

✶

I have learned over the years that when a parent receives a diagnosis for a child with anything out of the ordinary, there are many reasons why people around them are at a loss for words. Most of us have probably been guilty of this. Sometimes we just want to make it better. We don't know what to say. The truth is too painful, so we deny the heaviness.

Saying *it will be fine* does not make it so. I have experienced comments from people that feel insensitive, lacking empathy:

"God only gives you what you can handle!"
"Special kids are born to special people."
"It could be worse."
"At least..."

Often, those closest to us experience a sense of denial. Perhaps the enormity of it is too much for them because they didn't expect this either. In those early days, words hurt, leaving me to feel alone.

Rather than push people away or resent them, I wish I had been honest and shared how I was feeling. I discovered over the years my kids were much better served when the people in their lives attempted to understand the nuances of hearing loss, became better informed, and refrained from judging or offering unsolicited advice.

✶

When someone is unwilling to learn, it cuts. Take the time a neighbor watched my son while I ran an errand. While I was grateful for his help, something occurred that I've never forgotten.

When I returned to pick up my son, my neighbor said smugly:

"I think he can hear just fine!"

He "tested" my son's hearing and came to the conclusion Battle didn't listen because it was behavioral, and he was just using selective hearing.

This adult had no idea how hearing devices worked. All these years later, this experience has stuck with me because it was clear that some people just don't understand that people with hearing loss have to make sense of everything they hear, and distance or background noise makes it even more challenging. The ability to localize sound is limited when utilizing hearing technology; being able to discriminate between *meaningful sound* versus *noise* is also difficult, not to mention exhausting.

This is why someone who is hard of hearing may tune out information that seems unimportant to them. You can't simply just turn the volume up on their devices. For a kid who hears mumbling coming from across the room, it might not be perceived as meaningful, so they tune it out, as was the case in my neighbor's "test." But, when a child hears words that sound important, like *ice cream,* they are more likely to dial in.

Instead of challenging or judging someone's hearing loss, there are so many better ways to offer support to kids and their parents: Tell them you understand how hard this must be; Tell them you love their child unconditionally; Tell them you will be there for them; Let them know you will be by their side to support and love them.

It is then and *only* then…That it will be *fine.*

5

The Dreaded Whistle

Weeks after we exited the cold room with the news of our son's hearing loss, he received his first set of hearing aids. The truth is, I hated those hearing aids. There were several reasons for this.

First, there was a high pitch whistle the hearing aids produced when anything pressed up against them. I could not set my baby down anywhere or on anything without the dreaded whistle sound.

Before technology advanced, when hearing aid molds (the custom-fit piece of silicone that sits inside the outer ear) came into contact with anything like a car seat, a high chair, a bouncy seat, or the floor when lying on his back, they produced a whistle similar to a soft tea kettle.

Every time the whistle hummed, it meant my baby couldn't hear. Even if it was for a second, it filled me with angst, a constant reminder of how important it was for him to have access to the usable information the hearing aids provided.

✶

Then there were the ear molds.

They needed to fit snugly to work correctly and combat the whistle. Only, have you ever noticed how quickly a baby's ears grow? I can tell you—my son's ears grew crazy fast.

This meant weekly trips to the audiologist, located back at that city-sized hospital. The timing was critical when making new molds, working around naps, feedings, diaper changes.

We would circle round and round looking for

a parking spot, usually needing to nurse the baby in the car before hitting the bathroom for one more diaper change.

It was a game of hurry up and wait. Finally, into the bright room with the sticky chair. One ear at a time, I cradled him so the audiologist could get the gooey material into his tiny ear. I kept him still so the gel-like stuff would form properly. It seemed like an eternity for it to dry.

Most of the time, he cried, or wiggled, or both.

Once the timer was set, sometimes we got lucky, and he would fall asleep. Only then, the other ear: more crying, more wiggles.

As he got a little bigger, we used a system of double-dipping, a process done in the lab that made the molds a fraction bigger, so they would last longer. Once completed, it was another trip back to have them fitted to the hearing aids, but I quickly learned how to adjust the finished molds, so they could be shipped directly to our house, saving us a trip back to the clinic.

But there were more things than just the whistle and ear molds I hated about those hearing aids.

I felt jealous of other moms who had babies who didn't wear them. I wondered, *"What was that like?"* My baby had hearing aids; their babies did not. Mainstream mothering looked so simple to me. It appeared care-free. Whereas I felt overwhelming worry and responsibility, I imagined *those* parents shared none of the same feelings.

What's more, I cringed when a passerby would shift their eyes to focus on my baby's devices. I didn't want people to look at the hearing aids.

"Look at him!" I wanted to shout. His chubby cheeks, his pouty heart-shaped lips, his deep blue eyes, his cute new onesie, his beautiful heart. See *him*: ALL OF HIM!

I created a story in my mind, imagining people didn't see him; rather, they only saw the hearing aids.

✶

In the beginning, I hated those hearing aids, the hearing tests, the whistle, the stares. And in retrospect, I know most of those feelings stemmed from grief. Having a child who was born with hearing loss was not something I expected so there was no time to prepare for it. I had to hit the ground running. There was so much to do, and I didn't get time to accept the situation wholeheartedly. Instead, I just did what I had to do to advocate for my baby.

Secretly, I wished it were different. Like those moms I *imagined* were mothering the easy way. I buried the guilt and the shame for feeling anything but grateful for having a beautiful baby boy.

✷

Slowly, some of the fog began to lift as I became better versed in hearing loss. I developed tricks and systems to manage the hearing aids, the whistle.

Those moms I thought were so worry-free? I realized they had their own struggles. It became clear that mothering, especially a newborn, was hard for all of us. Hearing aids or not. I began to rely on the comfort of this sisterhood.

Even when the dreaded whistle was long gone and the hearing aids were replaced by cochlear implants, challenges still and always will exist. But so do magical moments. It's all part of the journey. When you are in the midst of the fog, struggling with comparisons, guilt, strolling your baby to and from appointments, speech therapy sessions, feeling all eyes on your baby's little ears...

I hope you will soon discover, like I did, that it is healthy to feel all of those feelings, not just the #blessed ones. The truth is, navigating any new path takes time, and parents with children who have hearing loss need to give themselves the much-needed grace they deserve.

6

Grace

When I was a kid, my mom backed our van out of the driveway, hitting my dad's new car, which was parked on the other side of the street.

My mom didn't see it; her van had so many blind spots. Perhaps she was in a rush or maybe she had a lot on her mind while recently dealing with some medical issues. After she hit the car—she was visibly upset and rattled. It was clear she couldn't believe she had been so careless.

But it's what happened next that I will never forget.

When my mom came back into the house and told my dad about it, calmly he said,

"Well, honey, that could happen to anyone."

Instead of responding with anger or frustration or disappointment, he gave her grace.

This extended grace would help carry her through overcoming those medical challenges and would soon be extended back to him tenfold, when months later he was diagnosed with cancer.

✶

I think about that moment in the driveway—when he could've made her feel worse than she already felt after backing into his new car.

Instead, he chose to be kind and, through example, showed his family what grace looked like.

The dents on the cars were eventually buffed out and made good as new. But that grace lived on. I continue to practice ways to give it to others. What's more, I'm learning how to give it to myself.

My hope for you is that you will tread gently and faithfully along your journey. Even when it's hard. Even when it's frustrating. Even when you feel as if you've messed things up and aren't worthy of reprieve.

No matter how tattered and disoriented you might feel along the way, giving grace to yourself and to others will carry you through and make some of the foggy patches feel a little bit lighter.

7

The Gift

I'll never forget the look in my dad's eyes when the doctor told him the cancer was sprinkled throughout his abdomen like powdered sugar.

It was in that moment I saw the man—who I had thought of as fearless—afraid.

What started as an exploratory surgery ended in an unspeakable diagnosis. It was the kind of news my parents needed to ask their three children to be excused from the room—so they could ask the doctor questions parents don't want their children to hear.

The fight of my dad's life began behind those closed doors.

Through chemo treatments and all the havoc inflicted by cancer, he never lived like he would lose the battle.

I think we all believed it.

What was more incredible: as his body began to slowly fail, his faith continued to grow.

Years later, after his year-and-a-half fight with cancer ended, I was given the most treasured gift.

I still don't remember how and when I received his Bible. But well over a decade after my dad's death, I opened it. His notes were everywhere. The most beautiful penmanship, written with his favorite black pen. Along with dates. Highlights. Underlined phrases, words, passages.

It read like a spiritual journey, now resting in the palm of my hands.

I carefully moved through the antique-like pages of the book, tattered from the years. He had

received it on his wedding day to my mother—
over 50 years ago.

Inside was a path.

The handwriting in the margins of the pages explained so much:

Why so many people at his funeral said he was their good—if not best—friend.

Why grown men had tears in their eyes.

Why my grandma (his mother) died suddenly, not long after his passing.

Why my mother never remarried.

Why all of our hearts were broken.

His life was filled with depth. He loved selflessly.

And now, as I flipped through the roadmap provided in Romans, John, James, Jeremiah…I know during the last months of his life, he was at peace. He knew—unequivocally—where he was going.

I thank my dad for giving me the greatest gift of these handwritten notes. They are like a cartography of this portion on the map of his life. I know he was at peace and lived a life which had a tremendous impact on so many. No matter what challenges I have faced, I know I can count on this *knowing;* it continues to lead me through the fog while also lending a hand to those who are in the midst of challenges of their own.

✷

    These lessons continue to impact and guide me. Some are expressed in small gestures he modeled for me, like slipping a piece of candy into my kids' lunch box or sending a friend a handwritten note of encouragement. Other times the roadmap he provided in that Bible and his life waft over me like a gentle breeze, reminding me to appreciate the symphony of colors in a sunset or a hot cup of dark roast coffee on a Sunday morning. Gifts are all around and all I have to do is open them up.

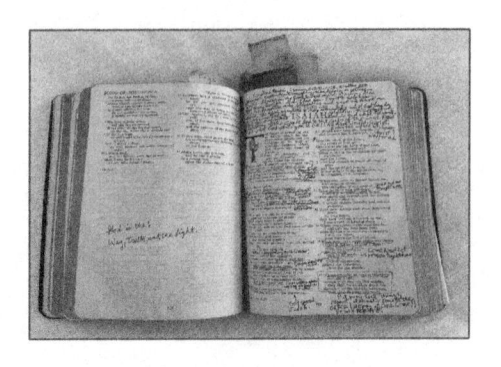

8

Eye Rolls

There was a thing about having a parent die in my early twenties. I often wondered who I would've become had *my dad not died*. This question haunted me for years after his passing.

I sat with him in his dimly lit hospital room, preparing to leave on a trip. I probably should've stayed, but he encouraged me to go. I had no idea this would be his death bed. I suppose in my naivety, I thought I could wish *this* outcome away.

I have never forgotten the phone call from my mom I received a few days after I left on that trip:

"Honey, Dad died."

For many years, those words punctuated what I saw as a selfish time in my life, the young woman I was at the time, the twenty-something year old I believed my dad knew too: the eye rolls, lacking any sense of humility, a know-it-all who talked more than she listened. He would never see me evolve, become a wife and a mother, or become who I was designed to be.

He was my mom's one and only. Her heart was shattered the most by his death, but despite her grief and pain, she somehow continued to show me grace as I moved through some rough patches full of mistakes, before landing at a place of acceptance and peace.

A few years after my dad died and I became a military spouse, I began to reflect back on my mom's life and my childhood.

Like the time I pushed my way through the open car door, leaping over the middle seat, throwing myself into the rear-facing third row of our 1978 baby blue Chevy Malibu station wagon.

"I call the backseat!"

"It's my turn," my sister declared.

Although deep down I knew it was her turn, I still proclaimed, *"But I called it."*

With less than a second to celebrate my athletic feat, a body landed on top of me. A few quick elbows and snarls later, I humbly crawled back to the center row. The bench seat. The dull and ordinary place in the middle.

My little brother, only 13-months younger, sat with his nose pressed against the window adjacent to me, asking hundreds of questions as he gazed out at the world with an insatiable curiosity. My mom patiently explained why the sky was blue and shared how the power lines provided electricity to power the lava lamp in our rec room.

Meanwhile, from the middle seat, I every-so-often flipped around to glare at the back of my sister's head. Two years my senior, she was not even looking out the oversized rearview glass.

Instead, she focused on the task of completing the Rubik's Cube faster than the last. She had made the front page of the local newspaper, solving it in record time. I secretly thought this was the coolest thing—EVER! In fact, I considered almost everything about my sister to be pretty dang cool. But…

What a waste of a good view, I mumbled. Meanwhile, I sat there quietly dreaming of how I was going to make own my mark.

Was there something to the perception of the kid in the middle? I'd heard the stereotypes and birth-order descriptions. Like the oldest is the bossy one and the leader while the youngest is coddled and gets all the attention. Then there's the poor kid in the middle who often feels overshadowed by the book ends.

Only, despite sometimes losing my preferred seat in the coolest place in the old wagon, I figured out how to turn the middle into the ideal spot. I mean, I got the benefit of both an older and a younger sib. And in my case, I had a brother and a sister. Most of the time, it seemed like a winning position. Being a member of a military family, relocating to far off places, I knew this sibling-thing I had going was golden.

Even now, as we have grown and evolved into adults with children of our own, I can't imagine life without being sandwiched between these two.

Growing up in a military family during the '70s, weekends on base were out of this world. After playing outside with a gaggle of kids in the nearby field, collecting branches and brush for fort-building, riding bikes, or skipping rocks at the quarry, all of us on the block would meet up at a neighbor's house once the streetlights came on. Plopped atop a sunshine yellow sofa, a gang of kids would gather around for a game of Sorry or Yahtzee.

I loved hanging out with the other military kids in each other's living rooms, olive-green shag carpet beneath our feet, while our moms sat around the kitchen table playing cards, drinking Tab, exchanging stories about life. My mom created a little slice of heaven for us while living on the base, located a short drive from the Sierra Nevada in California.

At any given time, half of the dads in the neighborhood would be away for a six-week rotation of Temporary Duty.

The people stationed on base became an extended family of sorts. We had a community of mothers taking care of us; their doors and hearts were always open. The ladies we considered second moms were Girl Scout leaders, nurses, at-home moms, and my heroes.

Growing up around these women was a treasure. I wouldn't even realize many of the lessons they instilled until decades later.

They taught me to treat every person with dignity, no matter what position or rank they held, and never act as if you were higher up in status than anyone else. I watched my mom and her friends embrace each family. I didn't know the difference between an officer and an enlisted service member until I was well into middle school because I never heard the adults around me discuss rank.

My mom and her friends were experts at transforming blank walls into homes. Whether it meant adding temporary wallpaper or creating a gallery wall of family photos, they quickly put their personal stamp on their new space.

I don't remember hearing anyone complain about a house being too small or the view being bad. Instead, my mom and her friends had a knack for making things work and being grateful for what each installation had to offer. They understood that a home was about the people inhabiting it with them not the quality of the kitchen countertops or bathroom fixtures.

My mom and the other military spouses I grew up around were gifted at the art of making friends quickly and relying on one another for so many things. If there was a crafty one in the bunch, she might help make the Halloween costumes, where a mom who had a teaching background might assist with math homework. This community of women was not shy to request or provide help when needed.

A welcoming culture, they formed inclusive horseshoes rather than closed circles. New families and old friends were welcome to attend impromptu cookouts, game nights, and gatherings on the block, all staples of growing up on base.

Early on I witnessed families helping each other pick up the slack during family separations. Whether it was carpooling or mowing a lawn, the entire neighborhood pitched in. If a mom got delayed or was in a pinch, there was always a neighbor's house to go to, raid the snack drawer, and hang out until the street lights came on. The families on base even attended each other's kids' ballgames, cheering loudest for the children whose parents were deployed overseas.

When Taps played over the base loudspeaker every evening at dusk, no matter what game we were in the middle of playing, base kids would hold the ball, turn towards the flag, and place our hands over our hearts until the bugle call was finished. The neighborhood moms reminded us to use words like please and thank you and to hold the door for others.

Decades later, Mom is still connected with many of those women she spent time gathered around the kitchen table with, many of whom also became widows. Families would come and go, but deep bonds were formed fast and forever. It is probably one of the most treasured and challenging parts about being a military family, saying hello and goodbye more than most people will in a lifetime. Unlike some civilian circles, military spouses pick right back up where they left off. Even when there may be decade-long gaps or continents between them, it's a tie that is hard to break.

What I remember most about my mom and her friends was a deep love and appreciation for service. They understood being in the military was much more than a job; it was seen as a calling and a privilege. The women in my mom's life didn't resent the military for the sacrifices endured by their families. They accepted both the good and the challenging parts of military life.

They proudly flew their flags and loved being Americans. It didn't mean they never struggled and found aspects of military life difficult. These outstanding women understood service did not come without sacrifice.

I think they were part of one of the greatest generations of military spouses. I was blessed to call many of them *mom*.

Rarely in the spotlight when it came to being on the receiving end of accolades and awards, I think being a military spouse suited my mom's understated personality. But the truth is, she was the hub that held the many spokes of our lives together.

This would never be more obvious than when I had children of my own; my mom was fast to acknowledge the magnitude of what it meant to have children who had hearing loss. Through all the hardest days, she showed up for me and for my kids, never minimizing the pain or lacking encouragement. Like the moms on base did for the kids I grew up with, she became my kids' biggest cheerleader. I'm sure becoming a grandma is what helped to begin healing her broken heart too, and I now know that my dad didn't need to live to be an old man to know who I really was designed to be; he could see the real me—beyond the eye rolls, he saw me. My mom and dad were both equally the greatest.

9

The Bean

Grains of grace I longed for began to surface with the birth of my daughter, who affectionately became known as the Bean. She was born perfectly petite.

It turns out there was more to this battle call, and even though we only had a lengthy list of boy names, we were delighted when we found out we were pregnant with a baby girl.

Harper would be her name.

Despite our firstborn baby being identified with having a hearing loss and all of the challenges that followed, the idea of having another child who would probably be born with *typical* hearing had us on cloud nine.

I guess I just glossed right over the 1:4 odds of a sibling also being born hard of hearing.

Whatever we were dealt, I convinced myself, we would just deal with it. We decided to wait until she was born to find out and go from there.

Then.

Three days before our first-born was scheduled for cochlear implant surgery, while four months pregnant with the Bean, we got the call. The routine quad screening results came back; it suggested she had a high probability for Down syndrome.

Naively, we hadn't even asked what our baby was being tested for. It was *routine*, after all.

We decided not to wait to find out. We wanted to know. Then, we could be prepared for… whatever.

That meant there was a silver lining. Now, opting for an amniocentesis, we could also do the genetic testing to check and see if she had the same condition that caused hearing loss for our son. It would be easy-peasy, we thought. We figured we would have peace of mind that *this* baby would be born with typical hearing.

I don't even remember the procedure. I suspect I was too overwhelmed to comprehend it all.

Our unborn child did not have Down syndrome. The genetic testing for the other would take longer. Weeks passed.

Then the call came while I was in the car returning from an audiology appointment with my toddler—who had recently undergone the cochlear implant surgery.

"Can you schedule a time to come in for the results?" the soft spoken genetics expert asked. I pulled over. Sitting in a parking lot:

"JUST. TELL. ME!"

The rest of the conversation is a blur. An overwhelming feeling of grief ran through me from the inside-out. How could this be happening again? I knew what it meant: the doctor's visits, infant hearing aids, surgeries, the worry.

I didn't want to be a poster child for hearing

loss just because of how well-versed I was becoming in it. We were still living in a fog, recovering from Battle's surgery, adapting to a new, more complex hearing device, and now…we would have to experience it all over AGAIN.

I immediately began a process of grieving. The loss of the life I had imagined for her, for us. The thought of the big stuff made me sad. But it was the little things…

A baby in the bath or pool or ocean that could hear a splash, the rain, a wave. Little eyes that would track and turn to the sound of my voice. Hear a lullaby, a whisper, a bird.

I imagined taking a baby out, without stares from people trying to figure out why this little baby was wearing those huge things on her ears. The sideways looks.

I felt sad about not being given a chance at mainstream motherhood, the *normal* way. The motherhood I imagined was experienced by most people I knew.

And then Labor Day came. Our little Bean arrived. We rolled up our sleeves and charged on.

In retrospect, I am grateful for having that

screening, which led us to the genetic testing we wouldn't have done otherwise. We got to process our daughter's hearing loss before she arrived, before we had to take any action on her behalf other than digesting the diagnosis. I was able to begin letting go of the things I had imagined, or wished, or longed for. And accept.

She was designed perfectly imperfect in a petite little package. She was our Bean and I wouldn't change a thing.

10

Rainbow Connection

One of the biggest challenges early on with having two children with hearing loss was how we were going to keep all these devices *on* these two active little kids.

When Battle and Harper were fitted for hearing aids and then cochlear implants, one of the messages we were told by hearing specialists over and over was how important it was for them to try to wear the hearing devices during all waking hours.

Well, I can tell you, keeping those cumbersome pieces of equipment connected to their pliable toddler ears was easier said than done. At times it was a battle.

Our MacGyver-like skills were put to the test daily. There was no Google or Facebook group to turn to for advice, because we are *that* old. We rigged up a series of contraptions: snug-fits which were a kind of hook that wrapped around the ear to hold the implant in place, plastic tubing which was cut and attached to the device then looped around the ear; toupee tape placed on the skin behind the ear so the device would stick to the sticky material, and ear molds inside the ear and attached to the device for additional support. We tried it all. My husband became an expert at the art of jury-rigging implants. Meanwhile, I developed a superset of eagle eyes.

And still.

Those devices would go flying off a bazillion times a day. Lost in the bottom of toy boxes, buried in stacks of pillows, submerged in the sandbox. There was even the time one was sent sailing into a bush inside a gorilla cage at the zoo. They would fall off, be thrown off, and the kids would carry on, leaving their implants in their wake.

Unwavering, we would put the devices on and bathe the kids in language. They would pull them off. We would put them right back on. Off. On. Off. On.

As frustrating and exhausting as it was to figure out *how* to keep the devices on, the trickier part was teaching the kids *why* they needed to keep them on.

Happy ear dances and songs were involved; it became a parenting style of sorts. I grew sick of my voice:

"I hear this. I hear that. I hear a bird. The bird goes tweet, tweet!"

The goal was to assign meaning to all sounds, often narrating in song and other forms of silly sound effects.

Chew, chew. Vroom, vroom. Beep, beep.

The car created a challenging scenario.

I couldn't keep my eyes on the kids' devices while driving, yet I didn't want them to miss the opportunity to listen to music, to sing. Inevitably,

61

a device would end up wedged between a seat or in a mouth.

Then one day it happened: *The shift.*

✷

When Battle was just a few months shy of his second birthday, while we were driving along, the external magnet of his device came off and he could no longer hear. The magnet cable dangled from his head, pushed against the car seat. Usually, this would trigger him to send it soaring across the car, stuck or missing…who knows where.

But, this time as I rolled up to a red light and glanced in the rearview mirror…

His little hand reconnected the implant magnet back to his head. His eyes lit up and were wide as saucers. He pulled the magnet off again. And then he immediately reconnected it.

A smile came across his little face, ear to ear.

"Yes," I shouted. *"Magic ears. You hear it!"*

It was as if the light had switched on for him. My daughter's version of an "aha" moment came later.

Oh, and that message about wearing devices during all waking hours…I soon realized it was something that might have sounded good in a clinical setting, but in reality, I allowed my kids to take short time-outs from device-wearing. This way I could have twenty minutes while cooking dinner and not have to keep my eagle eyes open and they could have listening breaks. Grace.

Even after the shift that happened in the car, there were still more scavenger hunts for lost devices throughout the house, car, playground. We had our fair share of implants pitched across the room. But my kids were beginning to associate wearing their cochlear implants with having access to sound.

We were making progress and starting to see a glimpse of a rainbow peeking through the fog.

11

Lost at Sea

Of all the places my children's hearing devices ended up throughout the years—sandboxes, toy chests, and a gorilla cage—when Battle was ten years old, a lost-and-found experience was hands-down the most miraculous.

On day two of a much-anticipated family vacation to Hawaii, my son's cochlear implant flew off his head as he played in the waves. It vanished.

His device was tucked securely in a new aqua-safe case designed to keep the cochlear implant dry while in the water. Recently developed by the implant company, this was a new tool for him and one of the first times we were going to try it out.

Even though I was yards away on beach, I could tell by the look on my son's face that he was panicked. I hadn't even seen the device come off with my own eyes, but I still knew: it was gone.

My entire family combed the beach for hours hoping it would wash up. We were praying for it to miraculously appear. But there was no such luck.

The beautiful ocean we had enjoyed all day suddenly turned into an enormous stealer of joy.

The irony was that, in the past, my son didn't usually wear his device in the ocean because the risk of it coming off was too great, not to mention the old models of aqua-kits sometimes leaked, causing the device to malfunction.

This time in particular, though, he was armed with the newly designed water-kit and was having so much fun playing in the surf with his cousins. Despite the crashing waves, I let him keep his device on, enjoying the laughter and sound of the waves crashing on the shore, usually a part of ocean fun he missed hearing.

Now it was gone. Washed out to sea.

I spent the next few hours on the phone making the "lost" claim and attempting to get a new device approved and shipped to us on the island. I went to bed that night deflated because there was no way a replacement device would arrive before we flew home.

Even the beautiful Hawaiian sunset that evening couldn't wash away the sadness I felt about the missing implant. Only it was followed by the sun rising on what would turn out to be a wondrous day.

An old friend from back home on the mainland who happened to be staying at the same resort was on her morning walk and passed by an outdoor cabana while heading back into the hotel. She noticed what looked like a device sitting on an outdoor counter, wrapped in seaweed, smothered in sand.

Battle's cochlear implant had washed up on shore and been turned in to the hotel's front desk, but the staff weren't able to identify *what* it was or *who* it belonged to. It was an unusual-looking apparatus in a silicone case covered in artifacts from the sea. This was truly a Magic Ear.

This friend, also a mother of a cochlear implant kid, knew right away not only *what* it was, but also *who* it must belong to. She had seen on Facebook that our family had also traveled to Hawaii.

And here we were: On the same island, in the same resort, with the same hearing technology.

She sent me a message and just like that, Battle's missing device was returned.

✷

Isn't this how life works sometimes? Challenges come when you least expect them. Then there are days full of pure joy. Sometimes they both happen in the same day. You just never know.

A storm hits, followed by seaweed, and ocean currents, and angels. In the morning, sometimes hope returns.

If you are lucky, there will even be a miraculous return of a cochlear implant. What's more, amazingly, that device might even still power-on after spending a night lost at sea.

12

Magic Moments

There were so many magical moments we experienced along the way.

Only, these moments usually were nothing like the videos splattered across social media of cochlear implant activations or first-time turning on a baby's hearing aid.

Most children who have hearing loss do not experience a magical reaction the day they receive their hearing devices. I know we didn't. Here's what I have learned, though: the real magic moments often come later, in smaller yet no less profound ways.

They happen when:

Your child hears a bird.

Your child learns a new babble sound.

Your child keeps their device on.

Your child includes their hearing device in their school self-portrait.

Your child makes a new friend.

Your child learns how to put their own cochlear implant processor on.

Your child makes it through an audiology appointment without having a meltdown.

Your child auditions for the school play.

Your child looks up and points out the plane flying overhead.

Your child says or signs "mommy" for the first time.

Your child plays a new sport.

Your child's teacher reports that they are engaged and participating.

Your child learns to play an instrument.

Your child earns an award at school for hard

work and effort.

Your child learns Chinese.

Your child learns to sign, "I love you!"

Your child is happy and has self-acceptance.

✷

The magic will most likely not occur in an audiologist's office when a device is activated or turned on. As challenging as it might be after viewing other people's experiences, remember patience will pay off. Because there are a million profoundly awesome moments that will come.

The magic most often happens in the mundane.

13

Cancer: A Good One

There's no sugarcoating it. Throughout this journey there were (and still are) some less than magical moments and maybe because my dad was only fifty years old when he died of cancer, I felt I might get cancer, too. In fact, before I was even diagnosed, I *knew* I had it.

A year before my diagnosis, on a crisp November morning, I broke down into tears in the middle of a training run with some close friends. I had no idea why, but I feared I had "It." Something wasn't right.

Months passed, but because of gentle nudging from my husband, I finally made an appointment.

It wasn't until the end of that doctor's visit, I *casually* mentioned the strange symptoms I had been experiencing. She ordered some tests.

After a colonoscopy (because of my family history of cancer) and an upper scope, I was declared squeaky clean.

I let out a deep sigh. Maybe I was wrong.

While I was in the recovery room, the doctor who performed the procedure asked me what had prompted my doctor to order this scope in the first place. I shared with him the weird symptoms I had been experiencing. He suggested an ultrasound of my thyroid.

Weeks passed. I eventually called to schedule one.

Next, came a dizzying whirlwind. After the thyroid ultrasound was completed, radiology reported nodules, which led to a follow-up with an ENT.

I opted for a needle biopsy in order to expedite

the process. Needless to say, having a needle inserted into my thyroid gland was extremely unpleasant. Much worse than that, though? The hurry up and wait…

The phone call finally came: Pupillary Carcinoma.

Shocked, I couldn't believe it. We were on military orders three thousand miles away from family, and my husband was scheduled to leave again soon for another military deployment.

"At least it's curable. It is a very good cancer to get." Or so everyone told me.

So I guess I didn't feel entitled to be scared, or mad, or anything.

✷

Prior to the surgery to remove my cancerous thyroid, I asked a friend if she would take family photos for me. Secretly, I wanted to make sure my family would have a recent picture with *all* of us in it, free of a gnarly scar.

Weeks later, my mom hopped on a cross country flight to be with us (again). Because in a time like *this,* all I knew for sure is that I wanted my mom by my side (again).

The surgeon cut it out. I woke up with an incision across my neck and a silent fear: I have cancer. I have two kids who require so much—an advocate and full-time champion.

What if…?

Rationally I knew I had the kind of cancer that rarely, once removed, came back or spread to other places in the body. Because my dad had experienced a rare form of cancer and his not only returned unexpectedly, it stealthy invaded his abdomen, sprinkling abnormal cells throughout, I guess I didn't have a very trusting or amicable relationship with this disease. I guess I wasn't trusting rationality.

What followed was a series of deep lows. I felt like I should just buck up and get over it. Every time I traveled alone to the cancer center for countless follow-ups, I knew I should be grateful because I was one of the lucky ones who had the *easy one.* So many others I passed in the hallways or saw in the waiting rooms were so sick. Some were losing their hair and/or emaciated, others so weak they were unable to walk on their own. Those people were fighting for their lives, and I was not. I was one of the "lucky" ones.

Although during the moments in between every test, each time I awaited results from another blood test or another body scan, I didn't feel so lucky.

My friend persuaded me to return to her studio for a post-surgical photoshoot, this time being the sole subject. It became one of my favorite photos. Sure, the lighting, the hair ... but mostly, the newfound strength it took to show off my wound. That photo is on a wall in my dream walk-in closet, tucked behind the door for my eyes only. That is pretty much how I have kept most of my vulnerabilities tucked away too, the ones that continue to metastasize from having gone through something so life-altering.

Truth is: we *all* have scars; some are just more visible than others.

Cancer drops like a bomb into anyone's life who has it, and I would venture that we will never be the same once it lands. There is always fallout—emotional, physical, familial. It is never "easy." Not hearing the word, not having it, not what comes after. If we are truly "lucky," it's when we discover our empathy and that of others who care and who truly get us.

It took me years to comprehend the impact of my own diagnosis and that disease had on me—a realization of how much it changed me: first as a twenty-something who lost her father, then as wife, as a mother, all of me.

I had cancer. But, at least it was *a good one*.

14

Those Damn Boots

Some of my husband's military deployments kind of felt like having surgery. You are unsettled in the period leading up to it and then you wake-up feeling out of sorts.

And when you finally make it into the recovery room—you can't really recall what happened. Occasionally there is some residual pain, but it can usually be managed.

The months working up to the actual deployment is when the irrational behavior would kick in for me.

Those dirty boots in the middle of the family room floor made me so mad.

Only…it wasn't really about the boots. It's the knowing: What is coming.

After ten deployments, I was finally able to recognize it. Deep down, I know: I'll soon miss those damn boots. The whole process is hard—before, during, after.

A few months post-cancer, the deployment that followed was one of the most brutal ones of all.

It was then I learned I could be a supportive spouse while still being upset about the leaving part, cringing as flak jackets and helmets were packed. When's the right time to go over his burial wishes?

Once the ship sails or the plane takes flight, there's an overwhelming sense of loss. Then, slowly acceptance sets in.

When our kids were older, they experienced a new set of feelings. Having a greater grasp of the inherent danger, unexplained stomach aches or short tempers occurred.

Missed birthdays, holidays, vacations, games, Sunday afternoons. Often I was left feeling like I failed because I couldn't be both Mom and Dad, no matter how hard I tried.

These frequent deployments and separations meant I managed most of the things regarding our kids' hearing loss alone. Whether it was schlepping both kids to speech therapy, audiology appointments for their cochlear implant programming and hearing evaluations, or just trying to manage all the parts and pieces of their devices, the shouldering of the responsibility to ensure both kids had access to all the things they needed to thrive was a lot to carry.

It took grace, and often I misstepped.

Months would pass. Eventually, the anticipation of the homecoming began.

And then, by the grace of God, came the return. Dirty boots back on the floor, under one roof as a family again.

It took time to adapt, adjust, and acclimate to living as a unit of four rather than three. There was a transition.

If you rip the band-aid off the post-deployment phase, you will find it is raw underneath. Even though I know how the game is played, I am left feeling in shock and awe by it all. Because the very nature of it is hard and humbling, and to admit this seems sacrilegious. Shouldn't everyone simply feel grateful to have the boots back on the ground?

But the truth is, that's not the whole story.

I have been home doing all things and being all the things to everyone. He's been over there, being everything to everyone. Then, in the blink of an eye, we are back under one roof as a family expecting the shift to happen instantaneously. Only, it doesn't, and things aren't exactly back to normal.

The kids test all the boundaries. Once they have your attention, they make it clear that absence comes with a price. As the mama bear, I instinctively protect them because I can't forget the times I soothed their broken hearts to sleep. I have witnessed firsthand the wreckage of his absence, the aftermath of all the days, weeks, months he wasn't there. The home team had to march on, and now we have to figure out how to include the entire unit again.

Yet, we know my husband's heart hurts, too. This isn't easy for him, either.

"I've been gone for…"

✶

To put the pieces of our family back together, it takes:

Time.

Patience.

Grace.

Forgiveness.

All things hard to give one another because of the dream image of a Hollywood ending. We made the video, took the photos, and people around us think it is just that. But it is not.

Truth is, we pay the price of each deployment for months to come, once he's back in the house again. The missed moments you can't get back lead to the resentment, hitting like a Mack truck.

Post-deployment life is a series of he said/she

said battles that center-around the unspoken truths of anger at him for missing stuff (and then inserting himself into the routine) and his guilt for missing stuff (and not understanding his role in the routine for a period of time).

Me: "You have no idea what this did to me! You should understand by now that I am breaking."

Him: "When can I be a parent again? It is hard for me too. You criticize too much."

All we can do is move through it. Own it. Peel it back and accept it was hard.

This doesn't mean I wish he were not here. It isn't saying I don't want him to serve. It does not erase the fact that I am proud of him. But this kind of service has left a few wounds. Pieces of us are broken and need to be glued back together. Bit by bit.

The children have to trust this is not a temporary scenario. Believe he is here to stay. I have to count on him again. Give up control, release the tight grip I have kept to survive.

Power struggles will continue to come and go. Debates about parenting will ensue. There will be bickering over combat boots not put away. It is all part of it.

And we will survive, wading through the muck, coming out on the other side. We always have. Always will. This is a promise we made to one another, many years ago, as we passed through that military sword arch overlooking the ocean on our wedding day.

There are cumulative effects of a life full of missed moments and being left behind and asked to be strong and hold it together. Everyone has to find their way, and it isn't always pretty, but there is always an unspoken sense of relief. Because the truth is: not everyone is guaranteed to return home.

We eventually recover, feeling prouder, more resilient, and grateful for those damn boots back on the living room floor.

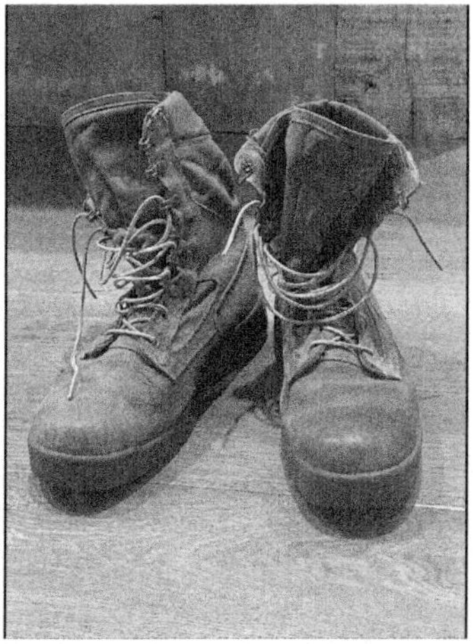

15

Hard Things

I had no idea how my training as an endurance athlete would prepare me for some of the challenges I would face.

Shortly after Chris and I arrived at our first duty station as husband and wife, I decided I wanted to run a marathon. Despite being an exercise instructor since the days of vinyl and leg warmers, long distance running had never been part of my repertoire. I'd spent most of my life cheering for my kid brother, JT, during his high school and college races. Running long and hard was in my brother's blood, taking after our dad, who was a collegiate national champion in track and field. I witnessed my brother training countless hours post-college for marathons. He was a natural. So much so he had a shot at the Olympic trials. The grit factor at this level was something to behold.

I'm still not sure why I picked up the phone that afternoon and called my brother to proclaim I wanted to run 26.2 miles. Perhaps I was homesick or needed to hear a familiar voice. Without hesitation, he offered to be my coach. But, he didn't sugarcoat it; it would take patience and humility.

The training was strategic, progressive, and required a one-day-at-a-time mindset. It wasn't a sprint; it was a marathon.

We picked the 21st running of the Marine Corps Marathon in Washington, D.C., for my debut race. A few days after that initial phone call to JT, a running journal arrived in my mailbox. On the inside, my brother had scribbled a heartfelt note of encouragement. Long before our daily emails or texts, we agreed I would call him every Sunday to get the training for the upcoming week and to report how the previous week had gone.

Anxious yet excited for this new adventure, I was off and running. My husband decided to join me on this new distance-running journey. On weekends, sometimes we ran side by side, or he would run ahead, looping back to pick me up. As the weeks passed, I learned about tempo runs, intervals, fartleks, striders, hill repeats. Before I knew it, I was up to two-and-a-half hour runs on the trails of the local state park. It was becoming enjoyable to put in the miles. For twenty weeks, I logged my minutes and kept track of my perceived exertion in my journal, slowly moving closer to my goal. By the time race day arrived, I was beyond prepared. I had done the work. I could step up to the line confidently with a plan; I could trust my training.

In spite of all of that…nervous energy filled me up from the tips of my toes to the top of my head, butterflies tickling my belly like never before. I had no doubt I was ready. But, even before the gun went off, things did not go as planned. As the pre-race singing of the National Anthem began, the skies of Washington, D.C., opened up, and a frigid rain began to fall.

With each mile, the torrential water soaked me like a wet blanket. Regardless of the less-than-ideal conditions of temperatures in the low forties and being very underdressed for the cold, wet weather, I had a skip in my step.

Chris and I were separated within the first congested mile, and I wouldn't see him again until long after the race was over. Despite being solo, I excitedly chatted with other runners along the way: a Marine who was carrying a flag representing his fallen brother, a group of moms who had trained together, a friend of a friend. Rumor had it, Vice President Al Gore was also participating in the marathon that day. I wondered if I was ahead of him. The camaraderie and enthusiasm among the participants were palpable. Countless spectators, undeterred by the rain, lined the streets from the Washington Monument to Arlington, passionately cheering us on.

All the nerves fell away as I settled into my pace. When I hit the halfway mark in less than two hours, an overwhelming feeling of elation washed over me: I was doing this thing! I wished my dad had been alive to witness *this*.

I was on target to make my goal time of sub-four hours. Approaching the mile 19 marker, I could hear her before I could see her. I looked over my shoulder and saw my best friend, Nancy. She was also running her first marathon, but we had agreed ahead of time to run our individual races since we now lived in different states and hadn't trained together. In a sea of over twenty-thousand runners, Nancy and I were side by side as we approached the infamous Marathon Wall—that moment when you've depleted your calories, you're dehydrated, and your legs begin to feel like lead.

My wheels were beginning to fall off. I had been running for over three hours and hypothermia was setting in, only my impaired mental state didn't recognize it. Nancy's survival tactic was to get chatty and tell stories, whereas mine was to retreat stoically inside my head. I had worked so hard. I had prepared. By mile 24, my shivering stopped; what few words I uttered were slurred, brain fog in full effect. The idea of holding Nancy back only added to my stress, so I told her, *"GO!"* I could tell she didn't want to leave me, but I insisted.

I shuffled on. Through my blurred vision, I thought I saw the Iwo Jima Memorial in view, the landmark indicating the finish line was near. Only, my legs began to buckle. With each step, the weight of each stride deposited more cement into both of my quadriceps. The next thing I knew my extremities were collapsing underneath me, giving way. Out of nowhere, two random runners grabbed me and helped me to the side of the course. I fell to the curb. Sitting hopelessly—frozen to my core—I could still hear the sweet voices of strangers running by, encouraging me:

"You are almost there; the finish line is just around the corner!"

After one failed attempt after another to rise to my feet, an emergency medical technician (EMT) appeared and assessed my situation. I could tell by his questions he was determining whether or not I required medical intervention. I attempted to "fool" him, only I couldn't remember what day it was or even my middle name. I was toast. Freezing, soggy toast.

A sea of runners rushed past me as I was placed in the ambulance. I begged the crew to let me out, to allow me finish.

"No one drops out at mile 25.5," I wailed.

After attempting to thaw out my defeated bones, drinking warm broth among other runners who were also gathered in the medical tent, my wits somewhat returned. I headed back out into the cold, feeling so alone as I wandered through a mass of thousands of drenched participants all wrapped in silver space blankets; I wept when Chris and I finally locked eyes from afar, miraculously reunited.

The days that followed were both physically and emotionally agonizing. I was filled with disappointment, playing over and over again all the ways I had misstepped, where I had gone wrong. Nancy felt horrible for leaving me, although there was nothing she could've done to stop what would become my fate that day.

The phone call to my brother later that evening was also heart wrenching. I felt as if I had failed; moreover, I had failed *him*. Only, in between my sobs, he kindly assured me that this was all part of endurance sports. You could never predict how things would go, the cards you would be dealt, and you just had to take the next step.

He encouraged me to pick the next race, dust off and place one foot in front of the other, and choose to toe the line once again.

A few months later on Father's Day, I joined thousands of my "closest friends" and did toe another starting line, this time crossing the finish line of the sunny, inaugural Rock 'n' Roll San Diego Marathon—with family and friends cheering us on for the entire 26.2 miles. You can bet Nancy and I stayed together from start to finish; she was the quintessential motormouth; I was mostly introverted. I felt my dad's presence on my shoulder when I hit the "wall."

The thing about doing bold things and exiting your comfort zone, the way endurance sports force you to do, is you don't know how it'll turn out. Even *if* you have a plan, do the work, there will be elements out of your control. And maybe you will not even understand the takeaways for weeks, months, or years.

I know after years of reflecting on my first marathon, even though I ended up with my rear end on the pavement a half-mile shy of the finish, I am still glad I dared to show up. It turns out *that* finish line wasn't the ending; there would be more races and more significant, life-changing moves. Some of those endeavors would have Hollywood-like endings, and some wouldn't go as planned.

Whether that's the letdown after participating in a much-anticipated event, being left out of a friendship circle, or being dealt a hand of cards you didn't expect, the truth is, sometimes you will need help from the folks in the emergency vehicle, and other times you will be able to remain on your feet. I took what I learned from the training process with my brother, and eventually became a coach for other aspiring endurance athletes, helping hundreds of (mostly) women discover and reveal what they were capable of achieving.

I had no idea that these things were preparing me for some of the longer, unexpected things, like having the kids born with hearing loss and all that entailed, but no amount of foresight can prepare anyone for everything.

Even after surviving cancer, being a military spouse, and raising two kids with additional needs, I sometimes haven't always felt strong enough to do all the hard things, even though I guess I have been challenged to do a lot of them. At times it feels like the perception by those around me is that I can and should have the strength.

I've never lost sight of the fact that my husband is doing difficult things, too. He is serving in harm's way, and that is incredibly hard. He is also missing out on everything at home. That is unbelievably hard. While holding down the fort in his absence, parenting alone…is also hard. As a couple, sometimes we are running side by side; other times, I am alone, praying for my wits to return.

It is all hard.

And so it goes…on and on.

Life just dishes out hard things. Always has, always will.

On a particular day I chose to set a boundary, I wondered if by saying no to something it might make me a little less gritty. Later that day, I was scrolling through some old photos and came across a gem. It was a photo of me and my boy on a vacation, right after we got out of the ocean from snorkeling.

His hand is placed on my shoulder as if to say: *"Mom, I am proud of you for doing a hard thing."*

I am petrified of fish. Despite being able to swim in open water in triathlons (I know, it makes no sense) the idea of strapping on a mask and swimming intentionally "with" the fish has always scared me. And not a little bit, but like *a lot*. But my son was so excited to do this, and I was in awe of him wanting so badly to do the thing that was so hard for me…

So I inched my way into the fish-filled sea. And the next thing I knew, we were swimming side by side, above a coral reef, playing peek-a-boo with a sea turtle.

My son swam lovingly close to me, giving me

an occasional thumbs-up, at times even reaching out to momentarily grab my hand, as if to say, *"I know it's hard, but I've got you!"*

And what is crystal clear to me after this experience beneath the sea:

Maybe I *CAN* do all the hard things. I just may *CHOOSE* to not always do *ALL* the hard things *ALL* the time. In life, we can embrace these contradictions. Like, we can acknowledge that having a child who has hearing loss is hard, while at the same time knowing that having a child who has hearing loss is also amazing.

Some days the amazing outweighs the hard. As parents, it is scary to hear about an initial diagnosis, but those fears don't mean we love our child any less. Saying we are having a hard day, week, or season does not mean we would change it. Nor does it mean we think our kids or our lives aren't whole or need fixing.

Just like it is possible to be a supportive, proud military spouse while also hating the "leaving" part. And the truth is, if we gloss over the challenging parts, we risk alienating others. Leaving out the difficult parts can make others feel alone.

Saying it's both hard and wondrous means we are human.

✷

It is fine to share portions of a highlight reel, the finish line photos and military deployment homecoming videos, but it is also brave to openly share the painful, less than picture-perfect parts. It's in the moments where I have fallen down and failed that I have discovered my resolute purpose. We don't always have to perform like a superhero to reveal that strength but (for the record), I later found out I would've crushed Vice President Gore's finish time had I not ended up on my rear end at mile 25.5 during that first marathon, so there's that!

We can be both—a fierce advocate who fights for all the things, and also a parent who is exhausted and occasionally needs a moment to gather themselves with some warm broth. Life is not a sprint, after all, it's more like a marathon.

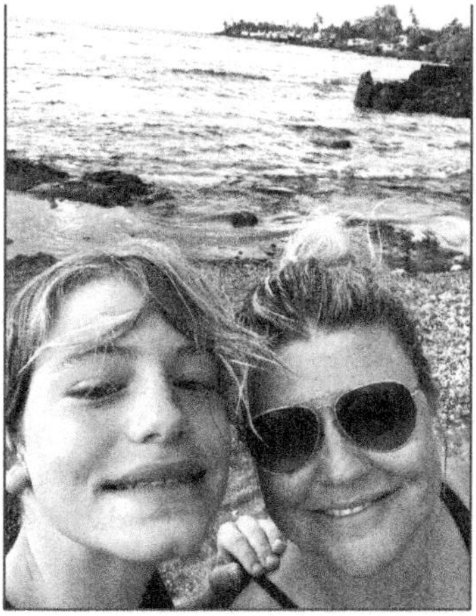

16

I Am Here

I waved the white flag and dragged myself into a therapy room.

A few weeks prior to showing up for that appointment, sitting at my kitchen table enjoying a cup of coffee in the quiet solitude of the early morning, I watched a video featuring an older man describing an encounter he had with a widow and how he "listened" to the whispers and shoulder taps of God. Out of nowhere, my fingers and toes suddenly began to tingle. I couldn't swallow. In a matter of moments, the beat of my heart began to accelerate. "What was happening?"

I jumped out of my chair and aimlessly paced around the room. Grabbing some water and trying to slowly swallow, I still couldn't clear the tightness in the back of my throat. I sat back down and took my pulse: One.Hundred.Eighty. "What was happening?"

My thoughts flashed to a story a friend, a few years shy of her fortieth birthday, had shared with me about when she had experienced a heart attack, punctuated with the fact that she did not even know it was happening while it was happening. Luckily, she went to the emergency room and lived to tell about it. Was this—*that?*

My heart still racing, tingling now headed towards my extremities, I paced again.

Poking my head into the room where Battle was engulfed in a video game, I asked him if he remembered how to call 911. Halfway looking away from the screen, he hollered, *"Yeah. Oh, wait! Why?" "Just in case,"* I told him in my nonchalant everything-is-fine-mom-kind-of-voice. I explained I wasn't feeling right…just kind of "weird."

I decided to take a shower because that seemed like a good thing to do when faced with a potential crisis. As the water began to trickle over my scalp, a headache hit like a pound of bricks. Flashbacks of my friend's story of her heart attack, was this *my* whisper? I decided I'd better head to urgent care.

It felt like an out-of-body experience as I wandered into the waiting room. Trying not to cause a scene, I stood in line behind a woman who was asking a list of trivial questions. I determined this was not a good time to worry about being polite and told the woman behind the desk something was wrong with me, and I needed to be seen right away.

With little urgency, she handed me paperwork and asked for my insurance card and ID. Trembling, I could not write, let alone open my purse. Now dialing-in to my unstable condition, she took me back to a treatment room for a series of questions and tests. The tears began to fall uncontrollably. "What was happening?"

The door closed, and I was left with a flood of fears. It was not a heart attack. *"I know it's scary,"* the medical staff member shared. *"Just try to relax,"* stepping out of the room leaving me alone to gather myself.

I calmly dug deep into a belly breath, as feeling slowly returned to my toes and fingers. I could swallow. The rapid pounding in my heart subsided.

What was happening was a panic attack!

The staff asked if I had been under stress and if this had ever happened before. I hadn't been…Or had I? But no, this had never happened before.

A few days later, I made the call I had been avoiding, canceling three times before finally showing up. After a heart-to-heart talk with my friend and OB/GYN, we came up with an action plan. One of the parts included talking to someone about some of the things I had made a practice of stuffing deep down. The cumulative effect of years of *sucking it up* had wreaked havoc on my emotional and physical self. For some reason, on this particular day when I sat in her office for a follow-up appointment, I let the truth come out. I shared how I had been lying to myself and those around me. I was not actually OK. Sure, I had let on about bits and pieces of my hurting heart, but I had yet to stare someone in the eyes and tell my whole truth—and allow for a person to offer a lifeline.

On this day, I did that. I welcomed the life raft.

✶

The following week, I met with a therapist and loved her from the get-go. She had worked with other military wives in the past and also understood the grief I was experiencing, stemming from losing a parent at a young age, the residual effects of having cancer, and the toll it had taken raising kids who have extra needs, often by myself. She gave me action steps, a plan that spoke to me on so many levels. Being passive in the process didn't appeal to my endurance athlete sensibilities. I wanted to actively work towards something. She gave me the tools to do that.

During our session, I recalled how, as a pre-teen, a gymnastics coach told my mom my I was too big for the sport. *"She has hips, a chest, and a waist,"* he said. That evening I decided to only have a slice of bread and water for dinner.

Next began the game of counting calories.

By my thirteenth birthday, my journal entries shifted from creative short stories to posts about starving myself:

JUNE~Today I only ate 500 calories! It feels so awesome, and I didn't even feel hungry. I hope Mom will buy me the calorie book this weekend.

JULY~I lost five pounds. All I have to do is watch what I put in my body, and I lose weight. My jean shorts fit looser than when mom bought them for me. And I can't wait to get measured for my cheerleading uniform and have the smallest waist on the team.

AUGUST~Dad sat me down and watched me eat a bowl of cereal because they are worried about my diet. So, I ate a few bites and then snuck to the bathroom. I have 4 pounds to go before school starts. I'll try cutting to 400 calories.

SEPTEMBER~Now everyone is getting on my

nerves, telling me I'm too thin just so I won't think I'm fat. But I see myself in the mirror. I know I am big. I just wish I could be skinny. No one cares. I need to lose weight.

OCTOBER~I am tired. I can hardly stand being me anymore. I hate my body. Not eating doesn't even work for me. I fasted for days and only lost 5 pounds. I wish I could be normal. I am disgusted with myself.

One of the things my new therapist encouraged me to do was return to the practice of yoga. Yoga had been something I had done beginning when I was pregnant with the baby I lost to a miscarriage while living in Cleveland. I credit this practice as truly saving me through a very dark time.

I continued to hit my mat for the several years that followed, through two more pregnancies, and the challenges they brought with two children who had hearing loss, while slowly turning that disordered thinking about body image around. Then, somehow my life hit some roadblocks. Something pulled me off the mat. Even though I knew deep down what a lifesaver yoga had been, I stopped showing up.

Which brings me to what happened after my first visit with my therapist:

I showed up to a *gentle* yoga class. In the past, *gentle* would never have been the kind of class I would have selected. But my therapist encouraged me to choose a more meditative, less strenuous class. Anything described as *restorative* or *gentle* would not have counted when it came to exercise for the former me. I mean, I had been an endurance sports coach, triathlete, marathoner, and hardcore exerciser since I was barely out of elementary school, and I had the leg warmers to prove it. *No pain, no gain* was ingrained in my DNA. But I trusted her. What did I have to lose?

The loveliest of instructors welcomed me to the class. We began the practice by setting our intentions. In a tone as smooth as butter, she encouraged us to select a phrase to say to ourselves; she encouraged us to repeat it if we found our minds wandering away from our mats. This was nothing new in many of the yoga lessons I had attended throughout the years, but for the first time I could remember, I actually set one.

As we began our breathing practice, starting to

flow, my mind immediately transitioned from the pose to judging myself, self-loathing the excess flesh I felt in poses which used to be elementary. My body didn't fold the way it had, just a few short years ago.

I stopped myself and silently repeated my phrase: *"I am here!"*

Over and over, I let my breath bring life back into my body. From the crown of my head into the roots of my feet, I kept repeating. *"I am here!"*

The practice finished in the traditional corpse pose. On our backs, eyes closed, tears began to flow down the sides of my face.

"I am here!"

I realized I had been speaking to myself in a way I never would have spoken to anyone else: put-downs, negative talk, toxic language. I imagined one of the women I used to coach, or one of the students in one of the exercise classes I had taught, or my sister, or a friend, or my daughter.

I would have told these women to give themselves grace. I mean really give it to themselves, to appreciate where they were today, not yesterday, not tomorrow. I would have encouraged them to be present on their mat in that precious moment.

My therapist was on to something. What I needed was more than just a *gentle* yoga class. I needed gentle self-care and to embrace myself by showing my body and mind kindness and honoring this place, at this moment, on this mat.

For the first time in a long time, I actually believed I deserved the kind of compassion I so willingly and generously gave to others.

✷

On this day, I gave it to myself. That single panic attack was perhaps "my whisper" designed to help me discover safe places, like a therapy room and a yoga studio, to continue to let go of the heavy things I previously stuffed down.

17

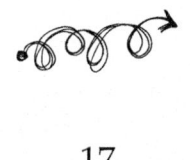

In the Trenches

Not long after that first therapy session, I was in the kitchen cooking dinner and overheard an exchange between my two kids—one whose voice was deepening and cracking and the other who seemed to be finding hers. They talked about things like Minecraft and TikTok, cutting up like two old pals.

I thought to myself, when did this happen? I swear it was literally yesterday when they were in diapers and cribs and highchairs and nursing and eating rice cereal. I carried a diaper bag, and my shirt was never free of spit-up. We were beginning our walk with hearing loss: hearing aids, cochlear implants, speech therapy, specialist after specialist.

How did this happen? I know I was there for it all, every moment. I have the stretch marks and worry lines to prove it. But how, in the blink of an eye, did I suddenly have two teens sitting at my kitchen table?

For anyone who feels like they are entering or living in a fog after receiving a diagnosis of hearing loss, I can share with you this:

It does get easier.

Sure, the challenges don't disappear. But the advocacy and dedication you are devoting to your child in these early years will reap huge benefits, as your child shifts from newborn to toddler, adolescent to teen.

I know your worry. I've felt it too. I worried about everything. The secret kind of worry, the things most people who have children born with typical hearing probably don't experience.

The truth is, I still feel a tinge of it once in a while, but it's no longer as razor-sharp as it was back then. Instead, I now find myself sharing many of the same concerns other parents feel raising teens.

The day will come for you when, around a kitchen table, you realize your child's resiliency and determination will carry them.

Rest assured, when it's all said and done, you won't want to change a thing. Even when things seem overwhelming—like you just can't handle one more hard thing because your heart hurts for your child—you will soon understand they were designed exactly the way they were supposed to be and you were made for this.

I can still remember wondering in the beginning if my child would ever develop spoken language or hear my voice. The thing is, I never really articulated my concerns. Instead, I tucked them away. But, deep down…I wondered.

As a hearing person, who had never met someone who had hearing loss before my own child, this worry was probably natural. I soon learned through technology and speech therapy, my kids could develop spoken language, in addition to the option of learning sign language. As parents, we made decisions based on the best information available to us at the time. The further down the road we traveled, the more it became clear: there was no *one* way to navigate this.

Today, there is so much more data and research available to new families who are starting this process. When our kids were born, there was some mixed messaging. That being said, we still remained open to pivoting and adapting our plan, depending on their unique needs.

Not every child benefits from hearing technology, nor is it the right fit for everyone who is born hard of hearing. The Deaf community is rich with culture and connection; some people opt for a combination of both spoken and sign language. There are also those who use one or the other. One isn't better than the other. Rather, providing a child with tons of love and access to language is key.

In the beginning, we started with infant hearing aids, extensive speech therapy, and later, cochlear implants. Our kids were meeting benchmarks, progressing, and exceeding expectations, but deep down…I still wondered.

The responsibility of ensuring my kids developed language weighed heavily on my shoulders and so did the secret worry. But with each magical moment, slowly the worry lessened. It was gradual. It wasn't obvious, even to me. It happened little by little. Then came a golden ring.

An early speech therapist shared with us in the very beginning stages—reminding us every week—the work we were doing today would eventually pay huge dividends; there would be a moment when the language would flow and never stop.

I wanted to believe it, but I couldn't imagine that moment actually coming to fruition.

And then one day, when my kids were barely out of diapers, we were driving in the car and I turned to them in the backseat and said,

"Can you two please QUIT talking for a moment!"

There it was: The golden moment.

Just like that. I didn't have to wonder any longer. Like cooking dinner and overhearing a mundane exchange between two teens around a kitchen table, magical moments are all around.

18

Maker of the Home

Not long after my husband returned home from another deployment, we went on a day date. Not the sexy kind of afternoon rendezvous where you order a glass of chardonnay someplace, feeling fancy. This was the grown-up kind of date, involving words like capital gains and deductions.

We walked into the office and took our spots on the vinyl chairs. The accountant pulled up our info on the screen and swiveled it toward us.

There it was, in bold print. Just nestled under my husband's name and title. Next to mine, read: HOMEMAKER.

My first reaction was shock. Next, I wanted to stand up and protest, but I suppressed my instinct to get on my soapbox. I figured it was best to just proceed with plugging in the numbers and get the heck out of this office. But there it was, popping up on the screen, over and over. Every time the accountant scrolled back to the home page: HOMEMAKER.

But, as I studied those 9 letters…I began to think. What did *that* title actually mean? Was *that* my job?

I guess I do make the home but perhaps not in the way that it was presented on that tax form.

I make the food: the lunches, potluck dishes, the cupcakes to share with the class. The birthday cakes, the family meals.

I make the schedules: sports practices, play-dates, football games, track meets, music lessons, clubs, summer camps, birthday parties, carpools…more birthday parties. More carpools.

I make the appointments: audiology, physicals,

well-checks, sick-visits, speech, orthodontist, ophthalmology, haircuts, IEPs, dentist.

I make the space we inhabit welcoming, warm, organized. I choose the towels to dry their bodies, the blankets to cover them when it is cold, the art on the walls to inspire.

I make the act of kindness a verb, showing them how to hold a door for a stranger, look someone in the eyes and smile, and include the person who is feeling left out.

I make the glue to put them back together after defeats, disappointments, heartbreaks.

I make the opinions they have seem valuable. And teach them when to be honest and when to bite their tongues.

I make their differences feel special and their commonalities unique.

I make the sky the limit and help the stars appear within reach.

I make the ordinary feel extraordinary and help turn the mundane into magic.

I make the decision to work from home a blessing; it is a gift, rather than a sacrifice.

I make the house a home, by ensuring the people who live here feel safe. Loved.

✶

Yes, I am indeed the maker of the home.

It's a pretty important position to fill. Whether you work inside or outside the house, or if the form has a different title next to your name, as a mom, you still do all the things to make your house a home. In the end, most of us are striving for similar things: Joy. Love. Home Sweet Home. Although my lines on the tax form have fewer digits next to them, without the maker of the home, all you've got is bare walls.

19

Rituals

Every morning my daughter and I used to do this thing. She would plop down on my lap while I sipped my morning coffee.

This particular day was no different. Each morning, my daughter asked me the same question. *"Mom, will you brush my hair?"* Without waiting for an answer, she would hand me the sage green brush that belonged to my dad.

Only, this time I almost gave her a different response.

For a split second, I felt the urge to encourage my tween-age daughter to do it herself. But I paused. Instead, I replied, *"Yep,"* while she had already taken her position, waiting for me to begin brushing.

As she sat, smothering me with her lanky limbs atop my legs, I carefully made my way through each tangle and snarled knot in her golden, sun-kissed mane. I was pretty good at making sure it didn't hurt; I sometimes wondered if she even realized that.

As I was finishing, she looked over her shoulder and asked, *"Can you keep brushing?"*

I did.

✶

In that moment I realized these rituals are fleeting. It wouldn't be much longer: she would brush her own hair; stand on her own two feet; and she would no longer be asking for my help in this way. It's not a matter of being capable of doing it herself. She'd done it plenty of times before. I knew, and she knew, she could do it herself.

But, these moments were much more than that. It was a morning exchange we shared that connected us.

I am glad I didn't tell her she needed to grow up. Because, as she was entering into this new season, her plate was becoming plenty full of things she did for herself. I was glad she still asked. The day was coming when she wouldn't.

The next morning, as we all buzzed around the house looking for this, packing up that—my son shouted from the top of the stairs:

"Mom, can you make me a lunch, please?"

For a split second, I almost hollered back up to tell him to make it himself. Flashback to the day prior and the green brush. Again, I knew he could make his own lunch. He was more than capable and, on most days, like his sister, did most things for himself.

I yelled back, *"Sure!"*

As I grabbed for the yogurt and raisins, I thought to myself what a gift it is to be their mother.

Doing for my kids is something I get to do:

I get to make their house a home.
I get to cheer for them from the sidelines.
I get to fill their bellies with nourishment.
I get to care for them when they are sick.
I get to take them here. And take them there.
I get to watch them grow and become.

∗

My kids were growing up so fast, with so many more responsibilities and commitments. They were able to do so much for themselves.

I remembered back to my own mom doing certain things for us kids and knowing how lucky I was to have such a nurturing mom.

In fact, one of my favorite childhood memories was when my mom would make us grilled cheese sandwiches with tomato soup for dinner. She'd deliver it to us on paper plates and bowls atop TV trays, while watching a show as a family.

Looking back, I am almost certain my mom did this on days the refrigerator and pantry were close to bare. What's more, these were probably days she needed a break.

I have moments when I feel I am not measuring up as a mother, or just doing too much for my kids. I try to remind myself my kids will probably not care about the gourmet, or organic, or fancy food they had or didn't have—or the fine china or paper plates they ate it from.

Instead, I hope they will remember who was there, gathered around, sharing meals with them, making memories.

So—I packed my son's brown bag lunch and threw in a piece of his favorite candy.

I knew as he sat down at lunch and reached in to find that little piece of caramel, he would probably grin. He would know his mom had his back. Even if my kids could do it all themselves, I get to be here to add a little sweetness to their day.

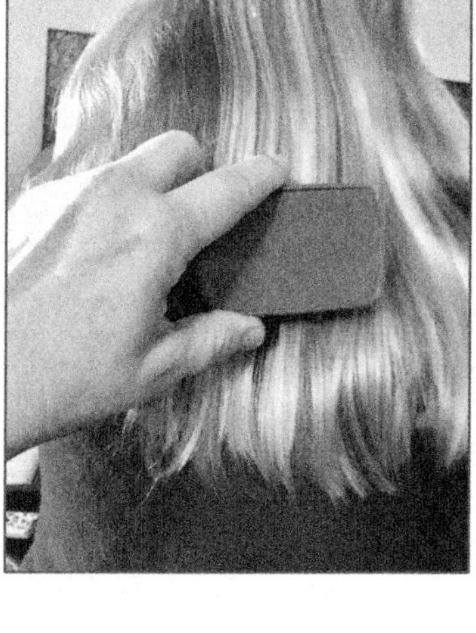

20

No Place Like Home

When we received military orders to Florida, I was heartbroken. I loved my life on the West Coast at our current duty station. I had a career that brought me an abundance of joy and purpose. My kids were connected and loved-up by family and close friends.

When we stepped foot in Tampa that midsummer day, the oppressive heat suffocated me while my heart melted, everything familiar disappearing. But, as most military families are accustomed to doing, we got busy unpacking and setting up another home.

The three years spent on the bay were full of many surprises, challenges, and unexpected curveballs. At times they were the lowest and loneliest, yet there were also blessings.

During that time, I was introduced to a circle of girlfriends who wrapped me in their arms and invited me into their world. I learned something really important about friendship.

Real friends show up.

They sit with you in your pain. They embrace you in your grief. They stay near amidst the discomfort, and love you through the hard. They rally around you and your kids in both big and small ways, in the darkness and in the light.

Real friends don't judge, give unsolicited advice, or try to fix it. They are comfortable in the stillness of the moment and in the middle of the storm.

They forgive you when you cancel. They never exclude or keep score. They are in it for the long haul, even when you are at your worst. They love your child like their own, accepting all their imperfections. They celebrate the victories and hold you through the heartbreaking setbacks.

Real friends aren't one-dimensional. They understand the seasons of motherhood, the ones that bring you to your knees. Yet they keep showing up.

Real friends are hard to find when you're in the midst of the fog, but when you do find one— and I pray you do—hold them tight. You may not find them in every place you land or in every season you find yourself. But the real ones keep showing up in the mess and in the mundane— and that's as real as it gets.

Of course, as fate would have it, we received orders to return west. After two deployments and a surgery for cancer, it was bittersweet leaving these women who had supported me in so many ways.

Returning to the place I had called home came with some unforeseen difficulties. It was as if we had returned home, only we felt like the new kids. Truth is, home is anywhere you build a community and grow. You literally can't go back.

Some people will disappoint you, while others will lift you up. And every corner of the globe has both kinds. I have learned this fact, often the hard way.

When I reflect back on some of the places God has placed us, the ones that seemed most difficult at the time were full of the most significant lessons.

✶

Take what some call the "Mistake by the Lake"—Cleveland. It turned out it would be a lifeline for our newborn-journey through hearing loss, having access to world-class experts. It was there I met a handful of people who would become my forever-friends. Ohio is where I also discovered the practice of yoga, which helped me get through my devastating miscarriage. When I got pregnant again, yoga led me to a prenatal class where I met a beautiful new-mommy circle of friends. The same women who were part of the sisterhood I leaned on while in midst of the fog. The ones who in the beginning I thought wrongly were mothering *the easy way.*

I know you can never really go home. Because the truth is, you are already there. I am pretty sure that's what Dorothy meant when describing the journey down the yellow brick road in *The Wizard of Oz*. It took me many moves, many tears, and many more years to finally figure it out. There aren't any mistakes.

21

Horseshoes

It was a new neighborhood, a new school, and my two kids were the new kids. We nervously arrived the first day of school, immediately passing a group of chattering moms who were taking photos of their kids wearing freshly pressed shirts, with newly trimmed haircuts.

As my kids and I approached the entrance, nerves palpable, we watched four moms—who appeared to be old friends—quickly round-up their kids for a group photo in front of the school marquee.

"I can't believe they've all been together since kindergarten," said the most vocal of the group.

They were part of a circle, while my military family was not. This was the third school for my kids and their friends were no longer classmates or neighbors; rather, their friends were spread across the globe.

I couldn't help but wonder what it would be like if some of those people were more willing to open their loop. What if one of those moms would've stopped to say hello?

That's the thing about circles and why a piece I read by writer Glennon Doyle—about the importance of not only noticing, but acknowledging those who are on the outside—resonated with me. She suggests forming friendship horseshoes (open) rather than circles (closed). It made me think about the people I've known and also how I have behaved, both in and outside of various circles.

I've witnessed those who are masters at including (like my mom and her friends, who lived on base), turning it into an art form. I've also seen others tightly grip their circular ring of friendships. This modeling spills over to the kid on the playground who won't allow the new kid to join in their game or the one who will offer up a seat at the lunch table.

I think as parents, we lead by example when we acknowledge the person standing off to the side, and we smile and invite them to join us.

I know firsthand. I've been the new kid. I have had the new kids, and I have also been a part of various circles. What each one of these experiences has taught me is that it is easy to focus on our personal positions and forget about others. I can't tell you how much a simple gesture means to someone feeling vulnerable. It can be life-changing.

✶

One of the best things that ever happened to me was *being* the new kid.

In the middle of my fifth-grade year, my dad's job as an Air Force pilot relocated us to another city. We moved during the Christmas break.

I remember entering my new classroom like it was yesterday. I walked through the classroom door, nerves raging, while the other kids reunited, gathering, excited to see each other after the holiday break. They laughed and caught up with one another, the way friends do when there's a clear familiarity. Just like those kids and moms at the school marquee.

That first recess was petrifying. I walked out onto the blacktop, searching for somewhere to go, something to do that would help me feel less alone and not stand out like a sore thumb.

It was shortly after I aimlessly wandered for what felt like an eternity, when one of my new classmates invited me to join in a game of four square. I nervously accepted. And within a week, I had a new set of friends (Nancy and Belinda, to name a few). They made room for me at their lunch table. They included me.

When I got married and became a military spouse, I experienced that *new kid* feeling over and over again. Each time we relocated, I hoped that one person would provide me with an olive branch—what's more, a lifeline.

There were some duty stations where I quickly felt at home; others proved to be less inviting. The common thread of the best ones was when at least one person went out of their way to invite me to sit at their table, join in their game. Those experiences taught me firsthand how powerful it is to pay it forward and be an includer.

It is this perspective that reminds me to notice the person who is searching the blacktop, longing for someone to make room and extend the ask.

✶

You may never know how much a simple gesture can help someone to feel less alone. Even when you are one of the lucky ones who is part of a circle, keep in mind there may come a day you become the one on the outside who needs an invitation to join.

22

To My Child's New IEP Team

As we entered my daughter's first Individual Educational Program (IEP) meeting at our new school, I thought it was important to lead with a different kind of introduction.

Before our meeting began, there were a few things I wanted the team to know about my child.

I knew we were going to discuss things like preferential seating, FM systems, sound-fields, and wireless microphones; we would address back-up hearing aid/cochlear implant batteries and create a plan for equipment failures. Closed captioning and audiovisual aids would be on the list of things we would most likely cover.

We would need to agree on whether or not my daughter would require extra time for test-taking and if she would be provided advanced copies of classroom notes.

These were all of things we would cover, necessary to ensure my child was educationally successful.

But there were a few things I wanted them to know, before we discussed all of her accommodations.

I wanted everyone to take a moment and remember my child was a typical kid who didn't have typical hearing.

She's more than her cochlear implant and her hearing aid. She's so much more than a diagnosis of hearing loss.

I wanted to share with them how funny she could be, how she's an athlete, and she'd never met a game she didn't like to play. How she loved being outside and would spend all day on her bike or skateboarding if she could.

Also, how she was obsessed with books, and if they turned their back for a second, they would catch her with her nose between the pages of an adventure story. A voracious reader, she'd likely finish a novel on the same day she checked it out of the library, and if they really wanted to get her attention, they could ask her to share some fun facts about Harry Potter.

In most ways, she was a pretty typical kid: fashion, music, friends. An enthusiastic learner, she'd likely ask her fair share of questions. Only, she might ask you to repeat a question more than once; she might not acknowledge you the first time you tell her something; she might not hear you correctly.

She might say, *"Huh?" and "What'd you say?"*

Please don't get frustrated. Simply repeat it. Because listening was hard work.

I would remind them to not mistake *hearing* with *understanding* because they were entirely different things.

Most of the time she would try her best, but sometimes she would just need a break.

I believed this IEP team cared about my child's well-being, so I would head into the meeting optimistic and ready to work alongside them, toward a common goal.

I trusted we wanted the same thing. The meeting was designed to ensure we all championed for my daughter's success. I would share the other stuff that wouldn't be part of the IEP meeting because it was just me trying to be a *typical* mom; I was a mom who, in addition to wanting the necessary accommodations for my child, wanted everyone at her new school to know she was so much more than the identification of hearing loss: *So much more.*

23

Dear Insurance Company

There were more battles to get through than just surviving IEP meetings and revolving doors of change. Having two kids born with moderate-to-severe hearing loss meant that without hearing devices, they could not hear more than a door slamming, drum banging, thunder roaring, or a freight train passing.

When they were outfitted with hearing aids at

three months of age, we were lucky that our insurance considered this a medical necessity and covered the cost of digital aids and regular audiology for programming, necessary to ensure their devices were programmed for each kid's specific loss.

We know not everyone is as fortunate in getting the medical care they need and while we can recognize that the people we talk to in the insurance office are performing a sometimes thankless job, being the parents on the other end of the phone when our children need help, it can feel like a David and Goliath situation to get the services we need.

We get impatient. We get frustrated. We want to tell the decision-makers behind the people on the phone what it is like. We want to tell them things like this:

If you haven't witnessed a baby in an audiologist's sound-booth being behaviorally tested for their ability to recognize sounds, you should check it out. It requires pretty amazing expertise and needs to be done repeatedly and with continuity.

Also, there's the re-making of ear molds. Because, you know what? Infants' ears grow pretty fast and steady. If the mold doesn't fit snuggly, there's this thing called "feedback" that continuously happens. Imagine the most annoying whistle sound, only the child hears little to nothing because the sound manager on the device cancels out all the usable sound. The user doesn't just miss the whistle sound but everything else too.

The thing about wearing hearing aids and having access to sound is that it is one of the critical ways a young child develops spoken language during the early years, when the brain is being developed and wired for language.

There's also the need to work with a specialist who understands how to help the child (and their parents) assign meaning to the sound they hear. For a child with hearing loss, this doesn't come naturally. For a child with hearing loss, science makes it happen.

So, again, although driving with a baby, two or three times a week, sometimes two hours away, to meet with a speech pathologist might sound like a fun thing to do…it's really not. But it is critical and necessary.

I stepped up during these incredibly difficult times because I believed that I was taking critical steps to ensure that the hearing aids we fought so hard for would actually benefit my child.

Now, here's the other thing…

Because of the nature of my children's hearing loss (the hearing fluctuates and is likely to deteriorate), they were candidates for cochlear implants. Not all kids benefit from a cochlear implant. What's more, some families do not choose this path. They utilize sign language, and those kids also thrive. As part of a deaf and hard of hearing community, most of us are OK with people making these very personal decisions to choose what works best for our families.

But when a child who would benefit a hundredfold is denied access to this technology because it is not deemed necessary by an insurance company…

Mama Bears get fired up.

For my kids, having these hearing devices has helped them to thrive in so many ways. I can't even fully articulate them all: academically, socially, athletically, and emotionally, to name a few. Our kids have been given the opportunity to do anything and everything hearing peers can do. You know—just be typical kids.

∗

So, as you may have gathered, as much as some people think a cute little pair of hearing aids is cosmetic or "elective" for the person with hearing loss, this could not be further from the truth.

Here's an idea…How about the people who represent insurance companies who see it as *nice-to-have* rather than *need-to-have* put a pair of earplugs in their ears for a day and go about their business. You may get a little frustrated when you can't hear the barista at Starbucks or have no clue what your colleagues are saying during your staff meeting. You will be exhausted by the end of the day from working so hard to try to hear. But, hey…just buck up!

Although our insurance through the military has approved everything our children have needed in order to thrive, many other families have not experienced the same insurance outcome.

Having a child diagnosed with anything out of the ordinary can be challenging. It causes strain on a marriage, tons of stress and anxiety for the kids and the parents, and then some. Throw in having to fight non-stop for the essential medical equipment needed to provide your child with the best opportunity to thrive, and you might find yourself on the ledge, ready to jump.

Covering hearing aids and cochlear implants provides families with peace of mind: *Let them know this is ONE battle they do not have to fight!*

24

Standing Ovation

Surviving the insurance-authorization process is just a small part of setting a child who has a disability up for success. In addition, at the end of the school year, there probably isn't an award ceremony for many of the things some kids accomplish. Their milestones perhaps aren't recognized as "achievements" in the mainstream classroom.

But I am here to tell you…Meeting IEP goals can be more remarkable than any certificate or plaque could convey.

Supporting new kids and welcoming and including others into circles is important, but celebrating the accomplishments of all kids is too.

Whether it was learning to advocate for themselves or exiting their comfort zones—I salute these kids. Not everyone understands how challenging their school day can be.

I applaud them for making it through bravely, doing the best they can. I acknowledge them for *SHOWING UP*—even when it was hard.

Maybe they won't be eligible for the "perfect attendance" award because there was the time they had surgery, had to visit a specialist, or other reasons outside of their control. But attendance is much more than simply being behind a desk every day. What matters most is what you do with the time you are present.

Sometimes they have to work harder than a *typical* classmate, but they don't use it as an excuse. They keep trying, without complaining, never feeling sorry for themselves.

The goals woven into the students' day can be exhausting and tedious. But they don't give up.

Because every day they work toward meeting goals—both big and small—students are becoming better and stronger.

There aren't many school awards for things like resilience and tenacity. So, when an IEP goal is marked as "achieved," they should feel proud to have exemplified those qualities that will take them far in school—and more importantly—in life.

I hope they know their advocates and champions are thrilled for them. Because most of us know: The things—often invisible—that require hard work and effort cannot always be measured, yet they are still worthy of a standing ovation.

25

My Battle Call

A few years ago, Battle and I were sitting at the kitchen table enjoying one of California's favorites, In-N-Out Burger. It was his fourteenth birthday, and since it fell on a weeknight this year and his sister had basketball practice, it was just the two of us. After some casual banter, he looked up with ketchup on the corners of his mouth, and asked:

"Mom, what was it like when I was born?"

Wow! The things you don't expect when you are in the middle of a birthday take-out meal. I smiled around my burger and shared the memory I would never forget.

✷

You were due on Thanksgiving Day. Only, you made us wait till the following Monday before you decided to enter the world. (At least it got me out of cooking!) But, boy, it was a long road leading up to that day.

When the pregnancy test came back positive, your dad and I were overcome with joy. Just a few months prior, we had lost our first pregnancy. We were elated to know we would be blessed with another baby.

Within days of finding out we were pregnant again, an early ultrasound taught us about things like a ruptured corpus luteum and the lack of progesterone. Our doctor told us she thought we could save this pregnancy. We saw no other option but to fight. This meant intra-muscular injections daily for the first trimester.

When I say you can be a pain in the butt—this literally started before you were born. It seemed like a small price to pay to give you a chance at life.

And in true *Battle* fashion, you beat the odds by continuing to grow and thrive. When we made it past the 12th week, we could finally take a deep breath and celebrate your impending arrival.

You loved to hang out near my ribs, and rocking and rolling was your favorite pastime.

I craved peanut butter frozen yogurt, but that wasn't easy to find in Cleveland. I settled for Taco Bell quesadillas and milkshakes. I taught spin class up until a week before my due date and my students made a habit of making fun of my big belly.

The day finally arrived. Labor lasted fourteen long hours.

I guess that's why they joke that women who give birth experience amnesia. Because what I do remember is that labor was harder than any long-distance triathlon or marathon I'd ever done. I'm pretty sure your sister wouldn't be here if I had truly recalled the whole thing.

Dad was super helpful from start to finish—holding my hand, feeding me ice chips, encouraging me.

I didn't say more than a few words. Grandma was by my side. I later found out that in between contractions, Dad was watching Monday Night Football. I think the Packers won the game.

When I heard your first scream, I was literally just thankful you made it through the birthing process. It's funny how much I worried about you even before you ever took your first breath outside of the womb. You were surrounded by so many people who cared deeply for you. It was then I knew that you would have an abundance of love in your life.

After the excitement of it all, when you failed the infant hearing screening, I wasn't even worried. I guess everything leading up to your birth just trumped the slim possibility it would be anything but *fluid in your ear canal* causing you to fail the routine test.

For two weeks straight, Dad and I just tried to figure out how to care for you. It isn't easy being responsible for a newborn. You were a huge eater, and loved having your burp cloth placed near your chin (you can thank Aunt Vicki for that trick).

You weren't a fan of the expensive swing we bought for you. Instead, you loved sleeping nuzzled on Dad's chest.

When we loaded you into your infant car seat for the follow-up hearing test on that cold, Cleveland morning, there was nothing more than a small sliver in the deepest crevice of my core that imagined you would fail it.

But here's the thing: as parents, you just don't know. The reality of what you will/might face once you have a child is much different from what you imagined. There is a plan much more complicated than you can envision. The news of your severe-to-profound hearing loss started the next chapter of the journey.

We were sent into a fog the days that followed. We tried to process it all.

After the shock of the diagnosis sank in, we had to accept it, then fight to give you every opportunity you deserved. Our one-hundred-year-old Colonial home had dial-up internet that was less than ideal when attempting to search for helpful information. Trust me when I tell you—our internet was slow as molasses.

You think I worry now? I am not going to sugarcoat it—the uncertainty as a new mom with a baby who was hard of hearing was plentiful. At times, I felt like I wasn't cut out for this life.

But as you sit here preparing to celebrate another birthday, I know wholeheartedly it was all perfectly designed. You have always looked to the planets and stars and reached for them.

While in the early days we wondered...

Would you learn to talk?

You not only learned how to listen and develop language, but you are also a motormouth.

Would you be mainstreamed?

The further down this road we got, the more I realized being "mainstreamed" wasn't important. Being included and accepted was everything.

If you want to know what a mama bear looks like protecting her cubs, just watch a mother walking into an IEP meeting. It is pretty much the same, only an actual bear might be gentler.

Would you play sports?

To think there was a time when we didn't think you'd ever pick up a ball. Now I watch you on the football field with an engine that never quits. Your athleticism is admirable because you've worked so hard to achieve it. It wasn't natural. It wasn't easy. But you never really have taken the easy route.

Would you make friends?

It turns out you're slow to warm up, even sometimes perceived as aloof. You lean into the people you call friends. Being the life of the party is not your style. I find your shyness endearing.

Sure, you exhibit all the other typical teenage things too. Your body odor is horrible. You sometimes forget to flush. Acne creams and toothpaste-scum line your bathroom countertop. Video games are king. You choose to sleep in at the most inopportune times. Sometimes your breath stinks and you interrupt. You occasionally say and do dumb things. Mostly you reply to our life-lesson lectures with one-word answers and grunt-like noises.

It's the sum of all these things that has helped

you develop a work ethic and resoluteness. Besides your tender heart, your grit is what I know will take you far.

Perhaps starting your life off having *this battle* gave you a unique view. Your experience has shaped your lens; you see life with an empathetic heart and have the instinct to root for the underdog—unless the Steelers are losing, because that quickly turns you into a fair-weather fan.

While a lot of parents dread the teenage years, I am entirely in awe of them. Maybe that's because you have exceeded every expectation we had for you as a tiny baby bundled, strapped in his car seat, leaving the hospital with a diagnosis of hearing loss.

The truth is—I can't imagine you any other way. Most of my worry has lessened, and I am left with hope.

What I didn't know all those years ago…is what being your mom would teach me about strength, resiliency, and love; it's the deepest kind of love you can only imagine in your dreams.

Through the fog, you will always be my *Battle call*.

26

To My Daughter

Dear Harper,

I love our car-music jam. So funny that that's where we share some of our best moments. Like how you can make me laugh with a simple look on your face or when we sing an entire musical soundtrack, from start to finish, at the top of our lungs. I love the way you sometimes still ask me to brush your hair or when you curl up next to me on the sofa for a binge-watch session on Netflix.

When I imagine the young adult you are becoming, I want you to know some of the ways I see you and what I also wish for your future.

Your body is a temple, beautifully designed as-is and does not need to be altered or changed to serve you. Embracing your strengths while allowing your vulnerabilities to shine through is important. It's not arrogant to have confidence.

I hope you will always have at least one friend who understands and accepts you just for being you. I know you have been that kind of friend too. Try to extend kindness. You may be the light in someone's life when you spread it.

You don't have to be "best" friends with everyone. Choose wisely when deciding who you surround yourself with. It takes practice, but you can avoid intentionally leaving others out by extending grace and compassion. Practice being aware and even invite those outside your circle to join. Reach out to the kid sitting alone. Make eye contact. Introduce yourself. Be bold.

Sometimes you're a homebody, so I hope you always feel safe within the walls of our home. I pray you learn to replicate this kind of security from the inside out and take it everywhere you go. When in doubt, continue to trust your gut.

Your grades and test scores matter, but your mental health and overall well-being are equally (if not more) important. Choose rest. It's OK to set boundaries and to say no.

Your mistakes are opportunities for growth. Being able to accept responsibility and to apologize when you misstep is something you already have learned to do so well. And when you put your foot in your mouth, you usually humbly admit it. Use those apologies wisely; back them up with sincerity. Make sure you mean it when you say it. Forgive yourself too.

Even if it's not trendy or fashionable, your uniqueness is golden. The older you get, the more you will learn, that in the long run, people care less about whether or not you are cool and more about whether or not you made them feel seen.

Like other moms and daughters experience, we have moods, and oh how they swing. Sometimes anger turns to tears, frustration becomes joy, often minute by minute. Take a deep breath and know some of this will pass. When you feel unlovable because you are displaying typical teenage angst, and you think I might agree (which of course I never could), I want to remind you that my love for you is unwavering, even when.

This next subject might be embarrassing to discuss with your mom. But, is it necessary? Yep. *Sex.* Try not to believe everything your friends say. Trust me when I tell you they are a little clueless on this subject, and probably most of them don't know what the heck they are talking about. Instead, keep asking me anything and everything, no matter how much it makes both of us blush. After all, I know a few things when it comes to sex because I've done *it* (at least twice) which makes me smarter on the subject than most 13-year-olds.

Then there's this thing called drama. Nobody has time for it; walk away from situations that don't serve you. But never be indifferent. Continue to speak up for those whose voices are softer. It's one of your beautiful strengths.

When it comes to social media: our house, our rules. You will thank me for this someday. Strive to get "likes" through real relationships. Friends aren't made to be collected by way of followers. Instead, work to keep making authentic ones. Remember, as your parents in this digital world, we are still trying to figure out a healthy balance when it comes to ALL THE SCREENS. I ask that you show us some grace.

I hope you keep exploring. Try a new instrument. Audition for another school play. Keep a good book handy. Understand things like math and writing are muscles; the more you use them, the stronger they will get. Keep singing out loud. Dance. When you feel down, turn your gaze up. If you find yourself searching for deeper love, take a knee rather than looking to empty, extrinsic places.

Finally, know you've been given many gifts, most of which will take you decades to realize. You will flub up and perhaps have some regrets. But keep trying. Embrace your failures and learn from them; it's all part of learning what makes you uniquely YOU!

May you always know being a teen is strangely amazing, and the best is yet to come.

Love, Mom

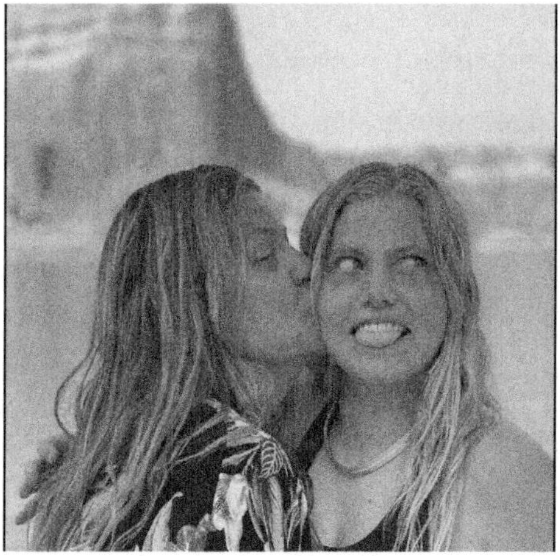

27

About Teens

I was talking to a good friend of mine who is a little further along in the parenting journey—hers in college, mine in high school—and we both admitted how few people we have to confide in about the struggles of raising teens.

I'm going to say something that might not be popular to say out loud, but it's certainly true for me. And it was for her too.

Raising teenagers sometimes feels isolating.

First, their privacy becomes super important. They don't want their business shared with others. It may be because it's embarrassing, or they just consider it nobody else's business. And that trust between you and your teen becomes sacred.

Next, teens are strangely complex humans. Most of them mess up (a lot). Not just in little ways, but in the kinds of ways that other parents at dinner parties whisper, *"Did you hear…? My kid would never…What those parents ought to do…"*

The stakes are high. We are no longer sharing tips and tricks about how to potty train or what worked for naps. The teenage years bring you real life, BIG issues and concerns. Actions and consequences can have a profound impact.

And the truth is, no matter how good someone's highlight reel on social media seems, there's no way anyone is getting through these teenage years without being a little scathed.

I'm super grateful I have a few close friends I can confide in when one of my kids is struggling.

I can also admit to those confidantes when I have made a huge parenting blunder, whether it's the amount of screen time (remember how we said our kids would never be on their devices that much?) or when I've lost my temper and made a bad situation so much worse.

※

One time, my son handed me a test, full of pages and pages of his work.

Instead of praising his effort, obvious from all the complex math problems scribbled throughout the pages, I skipped right past the work and fixed my eyes on the score. Then I said something like, *"I guess you need to study a little more…"* Immediately after the words left my lips, I regretted saying them.

His face went blank, head down and shoulders slumped forward, he turned and walked up the stairs. With my tail between my legs, I headed up to his room and plopped down next to him on his bed.

"I'm sorry. I was wrong," I confessed.

Surprised by my apology, he shared how this chapter was hard, but he was starting to get it. Truth is, I told him, I wouldn't have been able to solve even *ONE* of those problems that were scattered throughout his test pages. I admitted there's a reason I studied journalism and not mathematics in college. We had a good chuckle, then he jumped up and asked what was for dinner.

I've tried to continue this practice of owning up to my missteps. Because when my kids see me as a flawed human who admits my mistakes, they are more likely to own theirs, too. I certainly don't always get it right, but I try to admit when I get it wrong. Having the space to share these missteps with other parents who are in the trenches of parenting teens helps us all feel a bit less alone.

When you add to the equation having teens who have hearing loss, certain things become a little more complicated. Social nuances are more complex, and the transition to needing to advocate for themselves is paramount.

I actually have no idea how to fix this season of parenting that can feel lonely, except to find those select few who allow you to share the truth while also reciprocating by being an ear for someone else who needs to vent without passing judgment or thinking less of their kid.

The people I trust are the ones who can sit with me in our messiness and not see my teens as "bad." They allow for mistakes and assure you that much of being a teen is what they do after they make those poor choices, while also giving you grace when you get it wrong, too.

Being a teenager is hard. I remember it. The moods, the social dynamics, the struggle to manage it all while sometimes feeling like an imposter or that you are moving along a thin sheet of ice, just waiting for it to crack and swallow you up.

Grace. That's one thing I know we need during this season. We need it for our teens, and we also need it for ourselves and every dang parent who is doing the best they can. Give it. Receive it. And spread that grace generously around.

I've often said teenagers are unexpectedly amazing. I know this season will pass. As parents, we just have to hold on tight and lean on one another a little more—and judge each other a little less.

28

The Mustache

I only have a few photos of my dad without a mustache. I think he had to shave it off once (maybe twice) in his 27 years of service—for a formal military promotion photo.

He immediately grew it back. And never shaved it again.

I remember as a kid when he came home that day, clean faced, barely recognizing him. Because, you know…kids are weird like that. The funny thing is, he was a rule follower. But I think growing his mustache—just a little longer than regulation—was his rebel wink.

I mean, he drove on the highway the exact speed limit. He never rolled a stop sign. He pulled over for emergency vehicles. And got his cars registered and smog-checked well before the due date.

But that mustache...

What was it about that mustache?

He kept it groomed; however, there was often a crumb or two floating on the corner. Even though he was a very well-mannered eater. The crumb.

When I dream about my dad, his mustache is there. Right there. Crumbs and all. Only, he's usually flying up above, rather than driving in the slow lane. I try to imagine him now as an old man. Would his mustache be gray? Thinned? Or would he be cleanly shaven? No doubt he'd still be following the posted speed limit.

I imagine he would've made an amazing grandfather, instilling so many nuggets into my kids' back pockets. Like if you are five minutes early, you are late. How you should always do more than your fair share. When you see a problem, you own it, rather than pawning it off on someone else or expecting someone else to take care of it. You get up and help resolve it.

They would have learned from him the value of changing your oil before the light comes on and how it was better to fly fast and drive slow.

He would've taught them how roses from your garden are free and priceless and you should share them. How to be humble and how you should treat the person who bags your groceries the same as the CEO because relationships matter. That love notes are golden.

I am guessing he would've snuck a bowl of ice cream with them before bed because he believed it kept you young. He would've told them to put family first and love your spouse through your actions. He would've taught them to never doubt the profound mark you can leave during your time on earth. And last but not least…They would know cowboys aren't the only ones who can look cool with a mustache. I sure miss that mustache.

And I sure miss him.

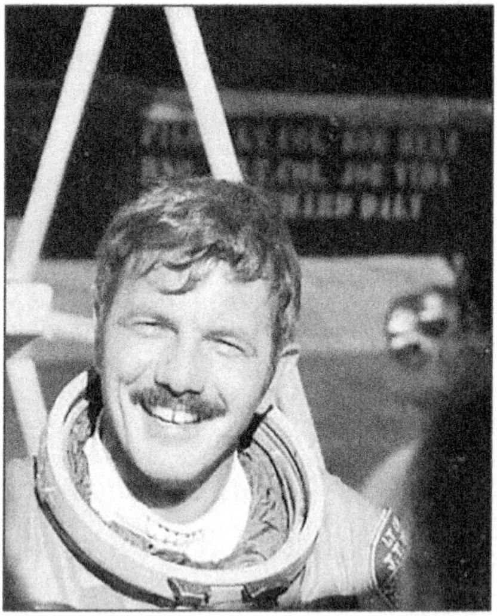

29

Perspective

"Enjoy it. It goes so fast."

When people use to say this to me, I rolled my eyes. It seemed so easy for them to say because their hands looked empty. Meanwhile, I was in the throes of balancing things like diapers and snacks, cochlear implants and hearing aids, chasing toddlers non-stop, having few moments to sit—let alone time to enjoy it.

While I was in this stage of parenting—everyone constantly needing something—the mothers of older kids seemed so relaxed, well-rested.

Life with littles meant no breaks from sunrise to sunset, loading kids in and out of car seats, managing moods, tantrums, and exhaustive sleep schedules. Not to mention the long list of appointments for speech, audiology, and the like.

Those days were long. Oh, so long.

Only, in the blink of an eye, there's a transition. I see a young mom chasing her toddler, hands full, and I realize what I didn't know back then is that those moms who whispered, *"Enjoy it"* were right. They were talking about more than just the heavy load of mothering littles.

Now that my kids are getting older, I realize there are so many things to enjoy about getting a little older.

You no longer care what people think. There is also less guilt when turning down invites, saying no to things that don't serve you, and sending regrets. You know who your people are and let go of those who aren't, and you are grateful for the things you have and no longer desire the things you don't.

You see, with age you no longer feel guilty when you can't return a text, email, phone call because you accept this new season you are in. You can go places alone without a hassle, like the grocery store or doctors' appointments. Your kids are old enough to stay home without a sitter or they can just wait in the lobby. Gone are those days when someone needs you every second of every day. When you go places, everyone carries their own stuff.

Nothing beats a hot cup of coffee, and you happily spend Saturdays with your kids because you have learned the days are long, but the years are short.

Those exhausting days that felt so long, fly by. What is universal, as your kids get older, is that you gain perspective, even though parenting doesn't become less busy. You still won't enjoy every part of it, but there are so many more opportunities to appreciate the experiences because you understand with each passing day these moments are becoming fewer and further between.

I still wouldn't tell a parent of small children

who is overwhelmed and exhausted that they should enjoy every moment of it; their hands are literally overflowing. But I might think it and smile a little bit on the inside. What I know now is the season of parenting young kids goes faster than you can imagine, even on the longest days. I didn't really understand that—until I did.

30

New Season

With every new season of parenting, we can either bend or break.

When my son was around fifteen, he chose not to put on his cochlear implants for the first hour or so after waking up. Unlike his sister, who reaches for hers the minute she jumps out of bed. They have their own preferences, and their needs are different.

I can't lie. Sometimes when he goes "device-less" it frustrates me a little bit—particularly when things are hectic:

"Did you brush your teeth?"

"What time is practice today?"

But, the older he gets, the more I have come to terms with the fact that, ultimately, he gets to decide how and when he uses his cochlear implants. Early on, cue the toddler years, we had committed to never turn wearing them into a power struggle. Still, this new stage feels a little bit different.

I think about the juxtaposition of this teenage situation and when Battle had just celebrated his sixth birthday. Soon after his surgery for his second cochlear implant, once the incision healed and the device was activated, he suddenly perceived his new external device as "itchy."

I managed to schlep the little guy to kindergarten, but Battle hysterically melted down outside the classroom door, vehemently refusing to put on his second device. It almost broke me.

Luckily we had access to an amazing Occupational Therapist who came to the rescue. After implementing a "brush-therapy technique," his negative tactile response to the new device dissipated, slowly allowing him to welcome what he referred to as his "baby ear."

Fast forward to the teenage years. I am literally relinquishing *power* over his use of his devices. As a mom, it's a hard thing to do as our children grow. We begin to gradually untether. We have to let them launch into each new stage.

He says he likes to quietly ease into his day. Sometimes when he comes home from a long day at school, he walks around the house without them on too. Perhaps it's his way of decompressing from the listening-fatigue of the day. It makes sense, and I am proud of him for discovering what he needs.

Regardless of how it makes me feel, as this boy turns into a young man, he gets to decide. The ownership is on him. He is behind the wheel. In this new season, I am becoming more of a passenger and trying to enjoy the ride.

31

Things I Learned Being a Military Bride

Oh, what a ride it has been. Minutes after I became engaged, someone asked me:

"Are you sure you can handle being a military wife?"

How the heck did I know what kind of wife I was ready to be? All I knew was I fell in love with a man who was a United States Marine.

I look back now and wonder how we made it.

Because what I didn't know all those years ago about being a military wife:

We would say goodbye to each other a bazillion times. But absence would make the heart grow fonder. And hand-written love letters would become golden. These separations would fall on all occasions: birthdays, holidays, anniversaries, weddings, funerals. But receiving my favorite flowers or phone message on the answering machine would make my heart sing.

We would learn about burial wishes, life insurance plans, and imminent danger pay. But after we cried buckets of tears, we would put our faith in God.

Our life would be full of things like military orders, having little to no say in where we went, or when, or for how long. But we would live in places we never imagined, often experiencing unexpected blessings. We would experience moving all over the country. First, finding a new home followed by packing and unpacking a million boxes. But we would become world-class organizers, fluent in making a house a home. We learned "things" didn't matter.

We would find ourselves outside of circles among people who had known each other since their kids were in kindergarten. But we would learn how to introduce ourselves. Initiate.

Our military friendships would not be defined by geography. They would be lasting. We would make good friends, sometimes ones that felt like family, at almost every duty station.

We would experience deployments and watch our kids' hearts break. But we would pick up the pieces. Because there wouldn't be any other alternative but to keep on. Our kids would learn about service.

We would not have the luxury of dropping roots in our favorite beach town on our own timeline, and my personal career might have to wait.

But we would learn to be flexible. And master the art of reinventing.

My husband would call me his center of gravity. Secretly, as the years passed, I would begin to believe it. Sometimes the sacrifices would be excruciating and at times seem unbearable. But, what I didn't know all those years ago is that in the end it would all be worth it.

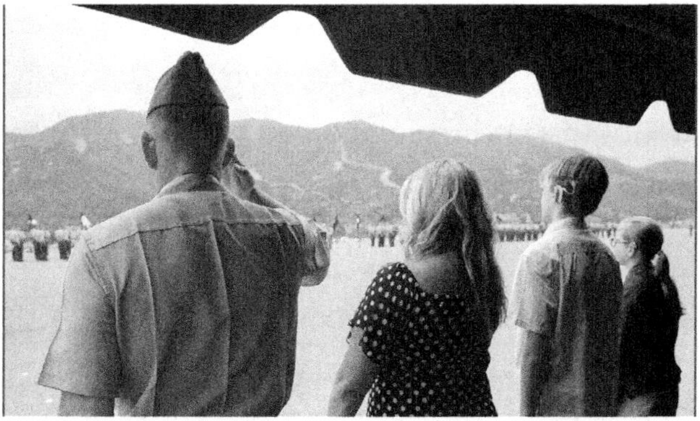

32

Dear Me

If I could go back and talk to my younger self, there are a few things I would want her to know.

When you find out your children have hearing loss, the feelings of worry and grief will eventually fade. Hang on, girlfriend. Yes, it is going to be challenging, and you will find yourself thinking you aren't made for this kind of stuff. But you will be OK. Your kids will be OK.

In the beginning, you will grieve the motherhood you imagined, envious of the friends who seem to be experiencing it *the easy way*. Those feelings will sometimes fill you up with overwhelming guilt because you keep hearing you should be grateful for having your otherwise healthy babies, that there are so many others who have it so much harder.

But you will move through the grief and accept your children are exactly who they were designed to be. These mixed emotions don't mean you have less love for your kids. Rather, it means you are human. You will learn you are worthy of grace, even when you think it is being withheld. The grace you long for will be unwrapped on antique pages, waiting to be discovered and uncovered.

I wish you could slow down while processing the unexpected nature of things before rolling up your sleeves and getting to work. You might be afraid of what the future holds for your kids. And you may worry whether or not they will be capable of achieving their goals and dreams because you have no idea what it will be like for them to grow up with hearing loss. You have no idea what to expect.

Only, you will soon learn—the sky is the limit. Hearing loss will not inhibit their ability to be excellent students, compassionate friends, and that they have an infinite amount of potential.

Brace yourself, because one of your kids will have his name called over a loudspeaker by a sports announcer after making epic tackles, while the other kid will share her own story in a children's book she'll write and inspire thousands of children.

They will learn to play multiple instruments, shred on snow skis down mountains, learn Chinese, and surf waves. Yet, there will also be seasons when it feels hard—really dang hard. But, those seasons will become fewer and farther in between. You will learn to put some of the hard stuff down and give yourself grace.

You will fight for your children's right to accessibility. Whether it's heading into an IEP meeting or refusing to give up when it comes to insurance, these battles will reveal a strength you never knew you had. Even when you hit the wall and end up on your rear end, you will not give up, rather you will dust yourself off, seek sunshine, and toe another line.

You will fear no one understands what you are going through, the gravity of it all. Sometimes you will find yourself on the receiving end of hurtful clichés. But some awesome people will show up for you.

Your own mom will always be a soft place to land and will come to you over and over again: Every time, no matter what, no matter how far. Your Dad will show up on your shoulder when you need him most.

You will surround yourself with compassionate experts who guide you through the process. You will create a team who ensures your children are not limited. You will learn who your friends are and make new ones, too. These circles will help you feel less alone; they will wrap you in their love. Some of these friends will become like sisters while your siblings will continue to comfort you, sandwiched between them like a warm blanket.

The man you married will stick through every crack, every heartbreaking season. Even when you find yourself running alone, you will be a team, no matter the distance, no matter the sacrifice.

But it's what your kids will teach you that will be the most profound. They will show you over and over again what perseverance looks like in the purest way. They will be resilient, adaptable, and empathetic. Because their journey will not be a typical one—they will develop courage. They will teach you that motherhood is an endurance sport and you will eventually sit back and marvel at how far you have all come.

While in the trenches, you will be overwhelmed by the choices you face and feel confused by the varying opinions of others. But you will learn to trust your intuition. It will lead you in the right direction. Whether it is a *knowing* feeling which leads to your own diagnosis or choosing the right therapist, your gut will often be right. Listen to it. Be patient because you will slowly discover this entire messy thing called life is completely worth it.

What would I say to myself all those years ago?

You have been given the opportunity to use the love of storytelling you discovered in a second-grade classroom to continue to share; you will have an opportunity to help spread awareness and make the world a more inclusive, tolerant place.

✶

This journey will be hard and at times you will feel like you are living in a fog, but if you hang on, light will always find a way through. I want you to never forget: *You've got this!*

With Gratitude

Mom: Thank you for showing me what right looks like and for showing me the way.

Vicki & JT: Being sandwiched between you two is a blessing; I couldn't imagine going through this life without you.

Christopher: I am so glad you chose to stick and never quit—and that I didn't make the 7 into a 9.

Nancy & Belinda: Thank you for giving me the courage to begin and for tolerating the countless hours of book talk. You two are the best friends a girl could ever have.

Dr. Joan Hewitt: Your support and encouragement through so many highs and lows has been invaluable. Thank you for always talking *to* the kids and not *at* them; they have always felt *seen* by you (and so have I).

Dr. Don Goldberg: You encouraged us to set the bar high and taught us invaluable lessons about having patience and finding golden rings.

Emma, Carrie, and Sherry: You were part of the sisterhood that saved me. You will never know how much turning your circle into a horseshoe meant to me. #pancakes

Veni: I am so grateful for the creative collaboration you lent to this project. Thanks for getting me to the finish line.

To the Teachers: Dr R, Mrs. Shem, and all of those who help kids believe in themselves and choose green ink. Your words matter and your impact is far reaching and life changing.

Jill: You truly are a *Blessing*. Thank you for your generosity and patience.

The High Time Habu: An American hero and even greater father, thanks for giving me so many precious gifts.

Glossary of Terms

Audiologist: A health care professional trained to evaluate hearing loss and related disorders. Audiologists use a variety of tests and procedures to assess hearing and balance function and fit and dispense hearing aids and other assistive devices for hearing loss. They also perform cochlear implant programming (MAPping). Most audiologists have advanced doctoral degrees.

Auditory Brainstem Response (ABR): A test used to assess the hearing of infants and young children or to test the functioning of the hearing nerve. The procedure involves attaching recording disks to the head to record electrical activity from the hearing nerve and the brain stem.

Bone Anchored Hearing Device: A surgically implanted hearing system that transmits sound to the cochlea (inner ear) by vibrating the mastoid bone (the large bone just behind the ear) instead of by amplifying sound directly into the ear. In young children, these devices are typically worn on a head band until their skulls are fully mature.

Cochlear Implant (CI): A device consisting of micro-electrodes that deliver electrical stimuli directly to the auditory nerve when surgically implanted into the cochlea, enabling a person with sensorineural deafness to hear. How it works: A CI is very different from a hearing aid. Hearing aids amplify sounds that a person can detect, whereas a CI bypasses the damaged portions of the ear and directly stimulate the auditory nerve. Signals generated by the implant are sent by way of the auditory nerve to the brain, which recognizes the signal as sound.

Cochlear Implant Programming: The process of programming the device, also referred to a MAPping, by an audiologist who has expertise in the field of cochlear implants. This is done in regular intervals. During the MAPping process, the stimulation levels of the CI's internal electrode array are adjusted so that the user can hear the wide range of sounds they may be exposed to.

deaf/deafness (lower-case): Partially or wholly lacking the sense of hearing.

Deaf (capital letter): Refers to persons who identify themselves as members of a community composed of deaf persons and others who share in their culture.

Deaf Culture: A set of social beliefs, behaviors, art, literary traditions, history, values, and shared institutions of communities that are influenced by deafness. Sign language is used as the primary form of communication.

Ear Molds: The part of the hearing aid that fits inside the ear and is customized to a person's unique ear shape. They are usually made of plastic or silicone and custom-fit so they sit snugly within the ear canal. They can have small vents to let air through.

ENT: An Ear, Nose, and Throat specialty medical doctor.

Hard of Hearing (HOH): Denotes a mild-to-severe hearing deficit.

Hearing Aid (HA): A small electronic device that makes some sounds louder so a person with hearing loss can have access to sound. It is worn either in or behind the ear. It has three basic parts: a microphone, an amplifier, and a speaker. There are two types of HA: analog and digital.

Hearing Loss: Partial or total inability to hear. There are three categories: conductive, sensorineural, or mixed, which is a combination of conductive and sensorineural.

Individual Educational Program (IEP): A legal document that defines how a school plans to meet a child's unique educational needs that result from a disability.

Microtia & Atresia: Congenital conditions affecting the development of the outer part of the ear (i.e., the pinna) or the external auditory canal (i.e., the ear canal). Atresia is no opening to the canal and microtia is no pinna/auricle on the outside.

Remote Microphones: Devices used to preferentially deliver the wearer/holder's voice directly into a hearing device. There are wireless microphones that utilize Bluetooth technology, personal FM/DM systems, and sound-field systems. For children, these are often used in classroom settings.

Sign Language: Method of communication for people who are deaf in which hand movements, gestures, and facial expressions convey grammatical structure and meaning.

Bonus Section: Feel the Love

Some encouragement from veteran parents of children who have hearing loss:

- Find a Deaf mentor. Connect with the deaf community. There are so many people in the Deaf/Hard of Hearing community willing and able to help.

- Find a great audiologist.

- Hearing loss doesn't define your child. It's a small part of them.

- Celebrate little victories.

- You are your child's biggest advocate.

- Teach your child also how to advocate for themselves (age-appropriately). Teach them to ask for what they need. Let them be part of the conversation.

- Make sure you expose your child to lots of words and books. Read to your child (a lot).

- Give yourself time to grieve but know this is not the end for your child. They can still achieve their dreams.

- There is always someone further down the road who can offer you hope.

- It takes time to learn ASL. Be patient. It's worth it!

- Find time to nurture yourself.

- Bring a notepad to appointments or someone to support you.

- As long as your child has access to language (sign/spoken) and love, it'll be OK.

- You will admire your child for overcoming hard things. They will be the bravest person you know.

- Give yourself grace. Take it one day at a time.

- Your child CAN and WILL move mountains!

What I Want People to Know About My Kids' Hearing Loss

- They are *typical* kids, who don't have *typical* hearing.

- If you speak in a quiet voice, they may not hear you.

- When they are in a place with background noise (outdoors, gymnasiums, restaurants, playgrounds, near the ocean) it is hard for them to hear.

- If they don't hear you the first time, don't get frustrated. Just simply repeat it. No need to shout.

- People who are deaf or hard of hearing make very different choices; there is not one way to navigate this personal experience.

- Avoid covering your mouth when you speak; they can't read your lips if they can't see your mouth.

- If you talk from across the room or with your back turned, they will miss most or all of what you say.

- If they don't hear you, please don't say *never mind.* It's hurtful and isolating.

- When the magnet on the device is off, the cochlear implant does not work, and they can't hear anything.

- Be patient. Frustration cuts. Kids who are deaf and hard of hearing often read body language better than the average person.

- Many people who are born deaf never know the cause.

- Listening with cochlear implants and hearing aids is exhausting. Kids need time to decompress, or they might act out.

It is harder than it *looks*.

- Understanding social nuances is really challenging when you are hard of hearing.

- They are resilient, adaptable kids, finding their way.

You Know You are the Parent of a Child who has Hearing Loss When…

Parents of children who are deaf or hard of hearing are a unique group of individuals.

Although there is no one-size-fits-all way to navigate hearing loss, there are many commonalities we share.

You know you are a parent of a child with a hearing loss when:

- You are more excited about your child receiving an upgraded hearing device than getting a new car.

- You let out a huge sigh of relief after a successful IEP meeting.

- You tear the house apart at least once a week looking for a missing device.

- You consider your speech therapists and Teachers of the Deaf (TOD) some of your closest champions.

- You bring tissues to your parent-teacher conference.

- You quickly know who your real friends are and appreciate the kindness of others more than you ever knew.

- You can spot a hearing aid, BAHA, or cochlear implant a mile away.

- You can change the batteries of a hearing aid with one hand, without looking.

- You point to your ear and say, *"I hear that,"* even when your child isn't with you.

- You have the cochlear implant company trouble-shooting department on speed dial.

- You celebrate when your baby makes a new babble sound.

- You get excited when your child turns toward their name when you call them.

- You feel happy when you don't get put on

hold with your insurance company.

- You are relieved when a referral or authorization goes through correctly.

- You are overcome with joy when your audiologist calls to tell you they had a cancelation and can fit you in.

- You can fix a broken device without any help from the manufacturer.

- You are overjoyed when your child draws a hearing aid or cochlear implant on their self-portrait.

- You go right up to another parent who has a child who has hearing device.

- You smile when your child becomes a motormouth.

- You have backup batteries in your purse, car, drawers, everywhere.

- You have found a missing device connected via the magnet to the refrigerator, car seat, or toy box.

- You advocate tirelessly for your child.

- You celebrate successes, both big and small.

- You believe in your child, wholeheartedly accept your child, and are proud of your child.

About the Author
The Mama Behind the Magic Ears

Valli Gideons is an author, speaker, and mother of two thriving teens who were born with hearing loss. With a degree in journalism, she transitioned from writing everyday stories to sharing her family's hearing loss journey. To date, her work has reached millions of people across multiple platforms. With an engaged community made up of parents and leaders in the field of the deaf and hard of hearing, she is passionate about her role as an advocate of children.

You can follow along here: www.mybattlecall.com
Facebook/Instagram @MyBattleCall

More by Valli Gideons

Valli's first book, *"Now Hear This: Harper Soars with her Magic Ears,"* is an Amazon #1 New Release children's book she wrote with her daughter, Harper.

Harper's story allows readers to follow her journey, providing both parent and child who are facing any kind of diagnosis a much-needed dose of encouragement. Through Harper's hearing loss story, kids can imagine what is possible. Understanding and awareness are the key to feeling included, and the community around a child with hearing loss is critical. A tenacious tween, Harper's witty approach to storytelling resonates with young readers while also offering inspiration and encouragement to anyone who has hearing loss or is facing any other challenge.

It's available on Amazon and BarnesAndNoble.com

Printed in Great Britain
by Amazon